SEL-LA-V

Life on the Earth

James Findlay

20. 9. 85

The Author with Roy, his black Border Collie 1954

JAMES G. FINDLAY O.B.E., J.P.

SEL-LA-V

Life on the Earth

The Pentland Press
Edinburgh

First published by

The Pentland Press
Kippielaw, By Haddington
East Lothian, Scotland

Typeset by Anagram Word Services, Edinburgh.
Printed and Bound by Clark Constable (1982) Ltd.
Cover Design by Ann Ross Paterson.

ISBN 0 946270 18 x.

CONTENTS

To my wife

SOME EARLY DOGS, AND A KILLER

I cannot remember any part of my life, except when in the Army, that a dog has not played a big part in my activities. The first dog at Mill of Marcus was a brownish bitch called Muss. I think it would be more properly called Miss, but when you are just two, pronounciation is more important than spelling. I think she would be far past her best by the time I turned up for I only recall her lying at the back door in the sun. The one I grew up with was a son of Muss's called Ned, a big black, white and tan fellow whose sire I did not know; probably no-one else knew either, but I think he must have been a reasonably good farm dog, because my father was choosy about things like dogs. He was a bit above average size, probably about 48 lbs; he had no style or eye; he barked when he thought it would have some effect, his brakes were much in need of re-lining — twenty yards here or there were not important to him, but the bold boy always got the job done in the time allotted.

There were no floats in those days and the fat bullocks were walked the five miles to Forfar with a man in front for the first mile till they were steadied down. Then he returned home, and his place in front was taken by Ned who regulated the speed and stood in any gate or side road till the cattle were past, when he would resume his place.

My father loved a shot of a winter's afternoon and Ned was daft about this sport. He did not carry, but he would kill a wounded rabbit or bird, and so earned his keep on such excursions. This was the activity that he concentrated most on when I got leave to go with Dad shooting. Ned and I had to walk close behind him and when waiting on rabbits to bolt, to stand close behind so there was no chance of being accidentally shot. To a five year old boy the time waiting for the rabbit to bolt after the ferret is put into the hole is really exciting and to see the victim somersaulting stone dead when at full speed generates a feeling of hero worship for the father who fired the shot. I well remember congratulating my father on a particularly fine snapshot and his reply is easy to recall. "When you are shooting well, Jim, you wonder why they are running or flying so slow."

In 1925 we got a new shepherd whose name was Stanley Dallas; the Dallasses have been famous shepherds for generations. There were five men altogether working on Marcus (some 200 acres) three

1

horsemen, a cattleman and a shepherd, as well as a serving girl in the house. Two of the horsemen were single and lived in the bothy, but most nights the married men were in for a crack and to get away from the bairns till they were bedded. Stanley had a mottled bitch called Fan, out of George Gilholm's famous Fan, and she was the apple of his eye, one of the new-fashioned "creepers' that people were beginning to go in for. Be that as it may, in due course she came in heat and to prevent Ned from getting her Stanley shut her up in an empty hen-house. Imagine his horror then when going to feed her one evening he found the bold boy lying beside her, both with expressions of wellbeing and virtue depicted all over them. Stanley went loco; you could hear the roars at Tannadice as he booted the indignant Ned out of the henhouse, then came straight down to the house and accused me of letting the big useless bastard in beside his pedigreed and valuable bitch — he had seen me playing in the cornyard after tea time — and demanded that I should be thrashed like I had never been thrashed before. My father asked me if I had done it and I said I had not, so Dad told Stanley to be quiet, there must be some other explanation. Stanley would have none of it; he said I must be lying and he wanted damages. He very nearly got damaged too for my father was quick with his hands, but the intervention of my mother saved him and he went off saying he would leave at the term.

Time, however, was then as it is now a great healer and in due course things returned to normal, and friendly relations were resumed. There is no doubt in my mind how Ned effected an entry. Every henhouse has a sliding bole which is pushed up in the morning to let the hens out and dropped down at night to keep them in till they lay. Ned must have managed to raise the bole with his nose — which ingenuity and ability was really an asset and highly desirable in the sire of any pup.

Anyway, one November day Fan had six pups in the coalshed of Stanley's house, and joy of joys, I was to get one. I was nine years old past 31 August. I picked a bitch with mottled legs like her mother, and practically lived beside them till we lifted her and took her home, not quite six weeks old. Dad wanted her in the house where the frosty nights would not get her and make her bandy legged, and where she would get plenty of milk and herrings — he thought herrings were the best thing to bring up pups on. Nobody spoke of proteins or vitamins in those days, but he knew their bones would be straight if they ate herrings and they would not be likely to take distemper.

Before I start on Pearl, I will finish up with her father. He was a confirmed raker and he taught his daughter as well. I have already said that when on walkabout they ignore commands to return and I instance Ned as a case in point. In 1927 we flitted to Hatton of

Newtyle — all 707 acres and four pair of it, and Ned and Pearl were part of the team. The herd there was the legendary Will Dick, a boyhood friend of my fathers, a tough little man. He always wore plus fours, and had the great blue strain of Nannie's all his life. This time Ned and Pearl had been absent for two days and Will came to the house at dinner time to tell us he had seen them on the Couston Hill and had got within 200 yards of them when they saw him and made off, though he shouted on them to stop.

"Did they not pay any attention?" asked my father.

"Oh they paid attention all right," said Will, "Ned looked over his shoulder, said shite and held going."

Will was really a tearaway, he loved a night in a pub and some of the stories he told me of escapades that he and my father got up to when they were young herding round Kirriemuir, could not be calculated to reinforce my belief that my father had always been a pillar of virtue and innocence. He had two sons, Jim and Martin; we buried Jim this year and Martin lives in Kirriemuir yet. One episode in Will's career sticks out the proverbial mile to depict the chap he was. When Jim left school and was leaving home for the bothy at the age of 14, Will did not shirk a father's responsibilities.

"Weel loon, I've brought you up as well as I could, and now I have to tell you how you should behave now that you will be awa on your own, and you'll be meeting new problems in life — so here's my advice — tak a woman whenever you get the chance but for God's sake bide awa fae drink."

I suppose there are folk like Will about yet, but I don't know them.

About this time my father interested himself in trials. I think he got the itch when we got friendly with George Skelton who had come up from the borders to farm Annagathel, and had the same dogs as his famous brother John at Burncastle. Skeldon's Geordie and his son Robbie were the dogs that were on everybody's lips in the early thirties and Pearl was taken to Burncastle and lined by Geordie.

I can see the pups yet, six again. They were kept in a pigsty at Hatton, and were of course all spoken for. You know how pups jump up inside a kennel to try to get you to clap them — well, five of the six did, but the sixth, a very sombre looking young man, would just sit at the back and look at you with his head to one side. He was the chosen one; we named him Barney and he was my father's constant pal as long as he lived. It will come to us all of course; one of our dogs will outlive us, and Barney was the one who outlived my father.

He was a tough little merchant, all Pearl's kind were, and a cat's life expectancy was about thirty seconds after Barney spotted it. Like his mother he disembowelled rats, weasels and even hedgehogs on the instant, and naturally the kind were too ready with the mouth on livestock. The little fellow could do very little wrong as far as my father was concerned. I mind one summer afternoon when we were dressing tups the racket got up round the corner of the shed, and when the old boy investigated there were his two dogs, Barney and Spark — the sulky one mentioned later — standing over the body of the newly killed cat.

"Spark, you are a dirty brute, and I'll lamp you till I'm tired", thundered the indignant owner — then to the repentent looking Barney, "Of course Barney I winna touch you, you would never kill a cat — in fact you like them."

I wondered at the time when Dad told me that before John Skelton fired Robbie he gave him a short bit of stick to carry which he kept in his mouth as long as he was working. The man was away ahead of his time; nowadays the wise ones say that a bark in an emergency is not a bad thing but they cannot bark if their mouth is full. Robbie's stick was his safety valve when the chips were down. If the new law banning gin traps is obeyed the following information will never be of use to anybody, but be it known that if your dog gets caught in one give him something to chew on when you are releasing him, for if you do not you will get your hand bitten whenever you touch the trap. The sufferer, in his or her agony blames you for the terrible pain and retaliates madly. Furthermore watch out if you have two dogs as the free one has a very strong urge to come to his pal's assistance. My father came home from the hill one day bitten by Barney on the hand when releasing him from a trap and by Spark on the leg when he was doing it. If you do not have a stick with you, throw your jacket over his head, hold it on with both hands, and depress the spring with your foot. Lastly, if you still get bitten, get medical attention at once; a dog bite is about the dirtiest wound you can get. My father lost the points of two fingers — a hard way to learn.

I have only once been bitten. It was a bitch named Flora that did it, and it was just one of these things. My father's uncle Charles Michie farmed Braco in Lethnot and my Aunt Jessie kept house for him. I was very much overawed by Charles; he had a black beard when no other body had one; he was very quiet and I always felt he was looking at me. This was when I was at the age of six or seven. He did not come home from the hill one day and the search party finally found him dead, guarded by Flora so determinedly that they had to get Aunt Jessie to come out and get a chain on her before they could bring him home.

My father took over Braco and put a herd in the house, and Aunt Jessie and Flora came to live with us at Marcus Mill. The bitch now transferred her loyalty to her mistress, and there were two things she would not let near her — me and Ned. She was always threatening us, and my father got angry at her. Ned would not sort her out although he was twice her size, but the end came when she bit me coming into the house one dinner time. The Marcus estate keeper McDougall was sent for and a No 4 from close range let her away to join her own master on the other side. Flora was unlucky; if her master had lived she would never have been in any trouble.

While on the subject of dangerous domestic animals, I recall one night when some of us were discussing the temperament of different breeds of cattle, and the Galloway seemed to be a short head in front of the cross-Highland as the breed most likely to kill or maim all but the most agile of humans. We were relating personal incidents and experiences and Ben Wilson — an upmarket edition of Will Dick — said it was not so much individual breeds, but families within each breed that needed special care.

"Nae doot the angriest cow in the Craigs herd is a Galloway", he reminisced, "Last year when she calved she gave the plooman a hell of a doing in, he was off work for seven weeks and then left. He was a lazy, useless kind of buddy, and he got just what he was needing — she has been ma favourite cow ever since."

One of my weekend jobs as a boy was to help the hogging shepherd to shift his lot from one farm to another. Between stock hoggs and sellers we wintered about 450 round about the coast, mostly near Arbroath and Dad had the wintering on about half a dozen farms. In charge was old Will Tulloch, from Glenshee in his young days, and he always put home good hoggs in the spring. A normal shift would be about 8 miles — as slow as you could get them to go — they should land full at night from the roadside verges. The big shift was on the 1st April when they went home, some to Braco and some to Hatton. On such moves thirteen miles was a big day and fourteen only in emergencies. The exciting bits of course were passing through towns or villages, with the local dogs either standing in the road holding you up, or trying to pick a fight with your dogs. I remember Geordie Coyne and me roading a flock through Kirriemuir, and Kirriemuir was a kittle place to drove through, when a resident dog assaulted Geordie's Garry. George strode over, reversed his stick and with one blow on the head, laid the attacker senseless on the road. His indignant owner having witnessed the scene from his garden, rushed over in a menacing manner, and confronted Geordie, but he was halted by his upraised stick. "One word out of you and I'll lay you beside him", spoken without any sign of emotion defused the situation immediately and the newly educated resident had learned in one easy lesson what I have said before: if you have a fighting dog you have to be a fighting man. There is another point

I would need to tell would-be dog owners in circumstances like this. If a strange dog introduces himself to yours, and they are verbally discussing the carelessness of each other's parents, it is fatal for you to call up your dog; for the instant that he turns tail his adversary will attack. If you just let them miscall each other for a short time they will invariably separate without coming to blows, and consequences like I have described above can be avoided.

Before I knew this I often put Ned in an embarrassing position on droves by trying to call him up, and he bore a grudge at me for it and refused to obey. It is maddening of course to see your flock proceeding into somebody's garden,and devouring their winter greens, while your dog is engaged in deep conversation with the local bully — probably the butcher's bull terrier. This day in Forfar just when I had got the hoggs turned into the Lochside Road to avoid going through the town, Ned took a long time to get away from a huge Alsatian and when he did come back I was frustrated enough to give him a kick on the rear. He immediately withdrew his labour, and just walked on the side of the road, absolutely refusing to pay any attention to anything I said, nor did he help me for the rest of the day. Today's people will no doubt wonder how anybody, let alone a boy of eleven and an old man, could walk 500 sheep fourteen miles in a day on the road. The explanation of course is that in 1927 if you met six cars on the main road in a day you were unlucky — four would be about normal, and as far as old Tulloch was concerned that was four too many. One thing though, car owners were mostly country people and knew how to pass or meet a drove. A motorist approaching a flock should drive right up tight against it as close to the side as he or she can get, to ensure the leaders are encouraged to pass. The best ones will also shut off their engine and exchange pleasantries with the drover when the flock is past. The worst ones will stop about forty yards from the point, lower the rear window so the terrier can shove his head out and bark, rev up his engine to the emission of black reek, while the five year old child beside him repeatedly operates the dual tone horns. Old Will had a stock phrase for such as these: "You are the worst driver I have ever seen, you shouldna be allowed on the road."

In those days one of the most important things in a dog was their feet — it is yet, but a day on the road could leave some dogs lame for as long as it took new skin to grow on their pads, while others could drove daily without ill effect. Try to get them with black pads and small feet, which appear to be far tougher than big feet with white pads. Pearl had terrific feet; my father used to take me in the morning to where the sheep were, then go on and drop my bike at our destination so I could cycle home at night with the bitch running alongside. She ran home to the Hatton from Braco one Sunday night, a distance of 23 miles, after taking the hoggs from Blackhall of Menmuir to Braco, almost thirteen miles, and was not a bit the worse. The kind of feet they have is easily discovered by letting them dig a rabbit hole, some will be lame in half an hour, others will dig all day and never make any odds.

The huge collie that killed scores of lambs in Angus and Perthshire in 1946 had worn his claws really short with constant digging, but the soles of his feet were like a new tyre. He held humans in supreme contempt and would kill lambs in fields guarded at every gate just to let us know what he thought of us. It took strychnine to kill him in the end, after he had defied hundreds of us for a winter and a spring.

His career created some interesting situations and some unfortunate events. At four in the morning one April day my herd Alex Baynes rattled on the window. I was just newly in bed, having been up all night at Eassie where he had killed the night before.

"I've got the dog" Alex shouted, "shot him dead just as licht was coming in. I want you to come up and see him."

This was right in the middle of our Blackface lambing so I was up at once. To get to the hill quickly I took my car because there was a road through Davidston Farm right up to our lambing bit. It was now about six o'clock and when I was going past Davidston steading Mr Horne the farmer was feeding ewes and lambs at the roadside.

"Great news, Mr Horne," I shouted, "Alex has shot the killer, would you like to come up and see him?"

"By God," said Mr Horne, "I will come with you, my dog went off last night and he's never got home yet." I got a sinking feeling, but hoped for the best. We motored as far as we could, then walked to where Alex was standing beside the deceased, whose entrails had escaped through the hole made by the soft nosed 303. Mr Horne, on witnessing the carcass, went absolutely grey, then started to shout using language which would have shamed a sergeant major of the Black Watch.

"You B's, you've shot my f.....g dog!" he screamed "You'll pay for this, by Christ you will," and seizing the beast by the tail he swung it over his shoulder and ran off with the dog's puddings hanging down past his knees.

He sued me for damages in the Sheriff Court and I counter claimed for disturbance to the lambing ewes. I was represented by the brilliant Archie Whitehead of McCash & Hunter and he took Mr Horne and his witnesses apart. The Sheriff found in my favour and awarded £ 26 plus expenses against the pursuer. The feud thus started and lasted all our lives — Fred Horne never forgave me. It is not for me to judge the rights or wrongs of this case but I think it was quite irresponsible to let a dog away on its own when lambs were being killed daily all round about, and that Fred and Fido got what was coming to them. He said my staff were not burying the ewes' after-births and thereby were attracting innocent scavengers. Fred is now dead; he was a hardworking man who I admired a lot, and if I meet him again later on I will try to make up.

The other incident worth recording in connection with the killer dog was one night when he was reported to have been seen entering a copse at Alyth Junction. I put four guns at points covering likely places for him to emerge and settled down to wait. About eleven o'clock a saloon car drew into one of the roads into the copse and a couple got out and went into the rear seat. I thought to myself: this should take about a quarter of an hour, I'll just let them be. However, after more than twice that time, as there was no sign of movement I felt I had to get them shifted so I approached the vehicle — windows steamed up as expected. I knocked on the rear window, and the chap screwed it down far enough to see what I wanted.

"I'm real sorry to disturb you when you're so busy," I said "but I think there's a dog in the wood that I would like to shoot when he comes out, so would you mind sitting someplace else?"

"Ach no," he says, "This is where we always come, we'll make a point of keeping quiet no to disturb him," and he closed the window. He was as good as his word, not a sound came from the car, though it was nearly one o'clock before they quietly drove off. I have no idea who he was or anything about him, but at least he did not have his priorities mixed.

One more think about the killer dog. I had a powerful spotlight torch taped under the barrels of my 16 bore gun lined up so that the shot followed the beam, so that I had only to illuminate the target and let go. I see that some inventor is making a fortune by selling a similar gadget to police forces — evidently the suspect offers no resistance when he observes the spotlight resting on his chest. When I read about this I felt I wanted to claim royalties.

Queer how I have diverged from discussing what kind of feet a dog should have to speak about lovers and lawsuits, but a day on the road was the thing to teach a stockman what kind of feet and legs sheep as well as the dog should have. The young herds of today are denied the compelling evidence that a sheep wrong ahint is at a terrible disadvantage compared to its fortunate brother or sister who is right ahint. It is because of this knowledge, hammered home by seeing the wrong ones practically needing carried the last mile while the correct ones were nearly out of sight, that my father's flocks and mine have always been particularly strong in this department. You can see the absolute truth of the need to have the muscles where they should be, and the bone formation suitable to co-ordinate with the muscles, if you watch any of our top jumping horses on the point of take off at a vertical wall.

In ending my introduction to my tales of some dogs I would recommend readers to enjoy again Burns' "The Twa Dogs." The bard had learned a lot in his thirty odd years about what goes on in the canine cranium. I think he gave Luath credit for more brains than I would have given him if his rudder is accurately described as "his gawsie tail, wi upward curl hang ower his hurdies wi a swirl." I am not fond of a collie with a tail like that; it is maybe all right for pulling sledges over the Antarctic snowfields, but it is not much help balancing a newly lambed ewe into a pen 5' x 5' set up against a hill dyke.

SOME DOGS I HAVE KNOWN

Of all the equipment available to the farmer no one item can be so instrumental to his efficiency or helplessness than the farm collie. For centuries they have been undervalued — we accept them as we accept our breakfast and seldom have to consider what life would be like if the kennel was vacant and the rattle of the chain on the flagstone no longer led us in the darkness of a winter morning to the usual welcome that awaits even the most undeserving masters from their willing and eager assistant. From this it should be assumed that the beast in question is worth of letting off the chain, for in dogs, even as in humans there are many that are not worth wakening in the morning.

We will therefore discuss before proceeding further some of the things in dogs that in the first instance separate the men from the boys, and the plusses from the minuses. Although I have never owned other than collies, every following observation applies to all breeds, and only varies in importance according to the purpose of the breed concerned. For example in lurchers, one that could run at 45 m.p.h. would be marginally better than a 42 m.p.h. model, but infinitely better than one that could only get up to 35 m.p.h. Any hare will verify that statement (in reverse of course).

Before we start choosing our particular dog there is one other factor that has to be borne in mind; he will adopt and develop the same character and personality as yourself, so a bit of self analysis is useful in order to prevent any doubtful bit about yourself becoming over-developed in your dog. Aggression is the obvious thing here that has to be guarded against, for the saying "If you have a fighting dog you have to be a fighting man" must be one of the truest of the various adages handed down from generation to generation in rural folklore. Nothing that I can think of can anger me quicker than to witness my dog, tired after a hill gather and bucht, being threatened by some useless brute that had just caused the last breakaway that took all that my dog could do to prevent an escape. I never hesitate to correct the offender with the full weight of my stick on his cranium, often to the verbal protests of his owner, whose father had not convinced him of the truth of the saying above. However, there are many things that make the difference between the aristocrat and the artisan and we must discuss and understand every one of them if we are ever to own a Millar's Speed, a Wilson's Nap, a Richardson's Cap, my own Roy or Fred, a Dickson's Hemp or a Taylor's Moss. I have not, and collie enthusiasts will no doubt have noticed that I have not, included in this list the legendary Home-Riggs Ben, but I really do not think there ever was the like of him before or ever will be again. We will come to him later on, but just now we will continue our discussion on characteristics.

One of the first has to be what should be the optimum sire of our super-collie and this is very important. A big one will eat more than a little one, he will rattle fences going through them and frighten his sheep, and will tend to be clumsier at tight turns. On the other hand his physical presence gives him initial power over domestic animals, and this can be critical at gatherings where sheep are strange to him and he to them. When catching a beast on a hillside his extra weight can often fell the quarry and save a long, weary trip to the burn and back again. Cattle especially have respect for size and a little dog is very much more liable to death or injury by attack from cows with calves.

It may be observed here that he could always run away from such an attack, but in my case this would attract the death penalty as soon as I got my gun. This weapon has to be very much borne in mind; dogs know instinctively what guns are for and many a good dog is reduced to a trembling dollop by the sound of a shot half a mile away. Although some strains have this disability in hereditary proportions it is my belief that every dog there is has some degree of susceptability, and a pup will turn gun-shy if he is allowed to see adult sufferers from this too common malaise. Conversely if he is kept in good company he will quickly overcome any initial uneasiness, and develop into an enthusiastic assistant at an afternoon's rabbiting or wildfowling: indeed some of mine would leif offer to go to help anybody they hear shooting if there is not much doing at home. Peter Gillon, the head gamekeeper at Pearsie and my friend, always instinctively starts to kick tins or boxes about when he is looking at any pup I have. "Get them used to the sound of bangs" he says.

This kind of treatment is certainly a big help, but it will never cure a dog of gun-shy parents, and a gun-shy dog will leave you on the hill with a hirsel half way to the fank, and will lie and shiver amongst the bales in the barn till dark, or even under your bed if he can sneak into the house when your wife isn't looking. So if we group together the ones that lie back off from suckler cows and the gun-shy ones, and eliminate them, and choose a family that is not too big to be clumsy and has not got a reverse gear we can proceed.

Nowadays with minivans, Landrovers and the like most dogs are expected on occasion to accompany their master from A to B and many, mine included, get into the house at evenings and mealtimes. It must be advantageous for them to listen to what is discussed round the fireside of an evening when other stockmen come in to pass an hour or two cracking about how the hoggs are doing or how they saw sixteen roughies on the south face of so and so's hill and how the milk clipping had been last week; or that two dogs, one a collie and the other a terrier had been shot yesterday having been chasing in-lamb ewes along at the Mains; or how a new shepherd was coming home to so and so with the reputation of having very good dogs and running them at trials. All the real toppers I have known are treated like members of the family so we must decide how best they fit in to the family.

As the only dog I ever knew who wiped his feet on the doormat before entering a house was the one and only Ben, we have to give preference to a kind that stay relatively clean even if working in muddy conditions. A short coated or bare-skinned dog enjoys a marked advantage in this respect; dirt does not stick to his hair, he dries much more quickly, and what dirt is on him is easily brushed off. He does not get immobilised by snow balling on his belly under certain weather conditions, he is able to dung without soiling himself and bees do not become entangled in his coat. His physical condition is much more easily assessed, so to my way of thinking a bare one has most of the answers. A close examination will often expose a soft undercoat on a bare dog; this is a good thing for insulation and body temperature control. There are of course numerous degrees of bareness or roughness but because there are plenty of good bare ones to choose from one should at least avoid really rough ones because of the disadvantages above mentioned.

Another aspect of this side of your enjoyment or otherwise of the company of your dog is his individual approach to personal hygiene. There are some breeds whose greatest ambition is to wallow in any kind of human or animal refuse and one of the most embarrassing situations that any owner can be confronted with is to witness his dog rejoining him and his guests with neck and shoulders covered with human excreta, which substance appears to rank highest of all the filth that rollers revel in smearing themselves with. If you happen to get possession of such a beast, and I have seen some otherwise decent ones, sell him to somebody you do not like because it will not be long till he does not like you either. A curious feature of this vice is that from the same litter some are rollers, and some are not, and they can be identified at a very early age. If you want to find out, just throw down a crow which has been dead about a week and you will get the answer within five minutes. No matter what potential a dog has, avoid rollers as you would avoid dysentry; there is no cure, and they will disgrace you at every opportunity.

Fine tuning in this characteristic is the body odour and bowel behaviour of your dog, as many dogs will lie on the rug beside you stinking like a midden day in day out, while the actual scent given off from their bodies could put the average fox or polecat to shame. My own brilliant young Ernest had a stronger than average body scent; you knew he was in the same room but his was so near tolerable that even if it was a minus it was so overwhelmed by all his other accomplishments that I began to associate his distinctive scent with his sky high intelligence and loved him even the more. I shall say more about him later.

One fault that cannot be recognised until too late is raking, that is disappearing for up to a week at a time hunting rabbits or some such prey. Boredom is the root cause here: a dog getting enough work will not go on the rake, but many of us do not have enough for our dog's wellbeing, and his instinctive desire to hunt will overcome his loyalty. Worse still he will entice away with him one or more of his kennelmates or neighbours, and apart from being absent when he is needed, and so exhausted when he does come home that he is useless for several days, the mental strain on yourself wondering what he is up to is almost unbearable and the asides from your pals at the next handling take a bit of living with. Again there is no cure. I have known a raker getting a number five in the rear from forty yards being back on the job inside six weeks. This is why we must discourage visits from neighbouring dogs. Although they assure you that the visit is purely social they should always be suspected of trying to get your young dog to go on the rake. If a dog disregards my vocal efforts to get him not to visit me, a number six at forty-five yards generally gets the message across, and he crosses you off his visiting list. This vice has nothing to with dogs appearing where a bitch is in season. Even the best dog you ever will own will desert you in these circumstances. It is natural and proper that he should act in this way and anybody that injures a dog attracted by the scent of such a bitch is either ignorant or evil or both.

Loyalty is a thing that deserves serious consideration in the dog's makeup, for an association that can last up to teens of years if formed from a base of affection and respect is much superior to one based on discipline and regimentation. To see Ernest almost bursting with joy when you complimented him on whatever he had just done, saying with every sinew: "Try me with anything else; I'll manage that as well," filled me with a warmth and wonder of such devotion and sagacity.

The difference of the two approaches were crystal clear at White Hope when J.M. Wilson had both Nap and Bill at the same time. The relationship between Nap and his master was very much the mailed fist — each was aware of the inflexibility of character of the other and having discovered which was boss, each accepted his role, as master and slave. Nap won his many trophies simply because he was an extension of whatever distance required of Jim Wilson's right arm. Nap was not anybody's real pal and I always thought he grudged being a dog and not a man. But when Bill was unchained it was a very different story.

William 1952

"Good morning, William," would say the smiling J. M. "Have you had a good night's sleep?"

Grinning from lug to lug the bold William would frolic round his idol assuring him that he had just enjoyed the best night's sleep of his life.

"In that case, William, you must be really thirsty. Why not run down to the burn for a drink."

Bill would set off at speed, take about 4 laps and return at even greater speed, like Ernie pleading on his master and friend to think of something else to try him with. Bill was not nearly as able as his illustrious kennel mate. At the time I thought he was not in the same class, but with what I have learned since I would reverse my placings because of the greater comradeship possible with Bill. If my memory serves me right, Bill did not get pups, but I believe that if J. M. only got one of his dogs to heaven with him, that dog is William.

Now that I have started to speak about individuals I will relate the story of the incomparable Ben. When, in 1939, I was called to the colours — I had been a Territorial soldier for two years — my father engaged an agricultural student and another herd to do my work on Hatton. The student was the highly gifted and distinguished Miss Adrienne Home-Rigg, and many were the glowing tributes paid her in the letters from home that I got weekly from my mother of how good she was at her work, and how nice it was to have her in the house, that she was really one of the family and really understanding about animals. My father let her use his own favourite Barney, while he worked with an unusually handsome dog I had at the time called Spark by J.M.'s Craig, a sulky brute that would never have been heard of in other than J. M.'s hands, and Spark was as sulky and dour as his father. To let you see how complicated the dog business is, my father who did the trials got far more prizes with Spark than he got with Barney (whose enthusiasm in front of other dogs invariably led to a loss of points) although he was not worth a hair out of the little fellow's tail. It was my rule that if a young dog did not come up to me for a reprimand about anything, I ran after them till I caught them, which was always at the house, and laid into them until they called me mother. This may seem to be cruel to people who don't know any better but it is actually kind, because it only needs doing once and your dog will all his life after come to you through hell or high water no matter the circumstances. I confess I have had two failures in my life that ran home when they thought I was angry at them even after the above treatment known locally as the long rope. I shot them both the same day.

My father died in 1941 leaving 707 acres and about 1,000 animals without a farmer to look after them and although I felt bad about it the powers that be brought me home from the Army, transferred me to a category W and told me to work on the farm by day and train the Home Guard by night. Having spent the last three years doing what I was told, I reverted at once to my earlier occupation. The dog situation was not good, Barney was done and going blind, and Spark and I never looked like getting on. I had sold a son of

Barney's when I was mobilised and his owner would not sell him back so we had to start again.

Adrienne and I decided to get a pup each from what was the ablest kind to be got at the time and were lucky enough to get two sons of Cap from Jim Wilson. They cost £6 each, were six weeks old, out of different bitches. When they came off the train at Alyth Junction in the same box I gave Adrienne first pick and she took the very serious looking Labrador-like son of Kirk's Nell.

"I'm calling mine Benny," declared the enraptured owner, "What are you calling yours?"

"Bruce," I replied, "I'm glad you let me have the collie."

Bruce became subject to epileptic fits before he was a year old and because I realised what Ben was, and that he might be triggered off into developing the disease by seeing Bruce in a fit, I had Bruce put down. From an early age it was evident that in Ben we had something different than what up to now we had thought collie dogs were. It was impossible to ruffle his majestic dignity and personality. He always wanted to help with whatever his mistress was doing, solemnly bringing her slippers from the scullery at tea time, wiping his feet on the mat before coming in, rolling over and over on command, like the children do on a grassy bank at a picnic. It soon became obvious that short of reading the lesson in Church on Sunday there was very little that the big fellow would not master and execute after one easy lesson. The ease and confidence with which he handled both cattle and sheep, his response to the various direction commands, marked him again as a God among mortals, he always gave the impression that he was not in a hurry but he never covered needless ground, was always in the right place and the job was over in a short time with neither beast or body breaking sweat. He was indeed a giant both physically and mentally, far bigger than what I consider ideal, but he needed his weight for some of the feats which I now propose to relate.

Probably the most spectacular of all was his ability on command to turn over sheep troughs and to turn every one over the same way. "Coup the troughs Benny" could send him a field breadth away and with paws and mouth he would lever over whatever troughs were there. "Show us more" the amazed onlookers would demand.

"All right then, but it looks like rain, Benny would you fetch my oilskin coat, it's hanging over the tup shed door." Carrying it over his shoulder like a fox carries a duck, the bold boy would soon appear to comments like: "I see it but I don't believe it."

About 1943 Adrienne decided to join one of the services to do her bit for the war effort and left me to look after Ben until her return. In the two years of her absence the big fellow was my constant companion and I added what I could to his repertoire. "What a lovely flower" I would observe, pointing to some daffodil or crocus, "Smell it, Benny, and tell me what you think of it." At once the great beast would approach the indicated plant, sniff it audibly and vigorously and joyfully wag his tail in approval of what he smelt. I am sure that he did this just to humour me for never did he indicate one that stank. He took a great delight in retrieving tups' caps which had been lost in long grass or in such crops as kale or cabbage, he would shut any door on command and open all but the ones with smooth round handles. I once shed ninety stirks — bullock from heifer — through a gate with Ben standing in the gap letting through the ones I told him to. Any reader who thinks he has an outstanding dog should try that sometime.

Because I could go on about Ben page after page and risk straining too far the credulity of my readers I will just tell you of what I suppose was Ben's greatest moment. The late John Black of Fisherton fancied his own dogs as the best that could be got, and had been telling me for some time that I would never be right until I had one of his kind. "My stud dog," he would say, "you have never seen anything like him; his speciality is putting bulls up trees." On this day when I heard we were having visitors including John to see the tups, I thought I would get his ideas into perspective. If verification of what happened is needed Bob Adam of Newhouse, Sir William Young of Skerrington or Jim Howie of Edglingston Mains were all present. For about an hour before their arrival I had been teaching Ben to take a packet of cigarettes out of my jacket pocket, which jacket I had hung over one of the cattle troughs in the shed where I had the tup lambs. Every time he brought them I told him there was not his equal and that before night his superiority would be universally acknowledged. I welcomed my visitors with a dram then we proceeded to inspect the tup lambs. After a few minutes during which time I had manoeuvred John away from the rest, the moment was right.

"Benny," I said, "I could do with a smoke, would you bring my cigarettes out of my greaser pocket."

At once the big fellow went over and carefully removed the cigarettes and came up to me in his usual unhurried way, wagging his tail ready for the praise he expected. I waited till he stopped in front of me. "Benny," I said, "where are your manners? It's visitors first, offer them to Mr Black," indicating that gentleman by pointing at him. You could have heard a pin drop as Ben walked over and held them up for John to take. Wat Taylor of Philorth was first to break the silence. "I'll give you £22.10s. for that dog" he gasped and Willie Young said, "I don't think you will get him." It turned out that on their previous visits they had decided to offer every farmer £22.10s. for what they thought was his best animal.

Adrienne came home and took Ben away to Kirklandbank, and after he herded there with her for some years, he finished his days in comfort and peace in the caring hands of the Misses Lindsay of Balintore. His place on Hatton was taken by his daughter Jess out of a stump-tailed bitch belonging to Jim Brown who always had good dogs — in Lanarkshire long ago the Browns of Borland and the Gibsons of Anston were the boys for dogs and all Jay Gibson's kind could kill a full grown fox. Jess inherited much of her father's sagacity and if she had lived long enough would have rivalled her grandmother Kirk's Nell as the greatest breeder of all time. She died after eating rat poison exposed after a gale of wind had blown away a sheet of iron I had covered it with. I phoned the makers in Surrey for an antidote but there was none. She only had one litter to a dog of Willie Bruce's of Balmyle, a big handsome son of McLeod's Garry, always bursting with energy, completely out of control. Willie had no idea how to handle him, but I liked him a lot. There were seven pups, every one a topper. The prettiest one, a black bitch with some tan from her father and bareskinned from her mother went to Troloss, but she was very aggressive on others of her age, and killed some poultry, so Ben gave her to his son-in-law, my close friend John Edgar of Skirling Craigs. John is recognised as one of the best handlers of dogs we have and Nell and he developed a relationship and understanding which will be talked about for generations to come, like James Hogg and Sirrah, or Adrienne and Ben, maybe even if my luck is in, like Findlay and Roy. Unlike her unlucky mother, Nell bred regularly for twelve years and her progeny were spoken for litters ahead. A lorry carrying a load of bricks reversed over her as she lay sleeping in the sun in the close and at the age of sixteen, full of honours, she rejoined her ancestors in whatever heaven is called in canine language.

I cannot go on writing about Nell for ever. John thought so much of her that he bred her pups brother and sister, and Skirling Craig will have dogs bred this way as long as there are Edgars in it. I lost temporarily the kind in a very curious way. I had got her daughter — a braw black and white out of Nell and by J.M.'s Roy, the fellow that had lost his tail somehow or other. She was a great favourite with us and likewise with Ben Wilson, who was always singing her praises, when he was up visiting. He used to say she was as sensible as her grannie and she was named after her, Jess. I was not really in the dog business and I was quite happy just to work away with her, my herds had good dogs and I was now more of a farmer than a herd. I was sitting in the house one night at the beginning of April when the phone rang. It was Ben but he did not have to tell you. When Ben phoned you held the receiver well away from your head, the power of his voice vibrated it like a tuning fork, and people in the scullery had no difficulty in following the conversation. Ben did not beat about the bush. After demanding if I was well, the next question was "How are you for dogs just now?" I was sure that he was about to tell me that he was sending two pups up on the train in a day or two, and as Marcus was an infant and I was over the head with work I did not relish the prospect. "Man, Ben," I said, "the place is crawling with them, there are nearly as many as on the place as sheep, your pal Jess will soon be ruined for the want of work."

"I'm glad to hear it," thundered the phone, "Put her on the train tomorrow morning — the hoggs are home from the wintering and misbehaving hellish — there's no a decent dog on Troloss just now and John will no give me a loan of Nell — you'll get her back next time I'm up." He had her for ten years — and I was out of dogs again. There must be a moral here about what happens to people who are too polite to say what they mean.

At this time the dog that most people liked best was Millar's Ben. He was a son of the great one out of Geordie Robertson's Jen, and Geordie had won the odd trial with him. When Jim Millar bought him and polished a bit, he became the dog at trials that the others had to beat and because of his likeness to his sire I decided to get into his kind. I answered an advertisement in the *Scottish Farmer* about pups off him out of Willie Ferguson's Jill and told him to send me two dog pups, the one most like a labrador and the one he meant to keep for himself. Imagine my joy when on opening the box there was the image of Old Ben himself, the smooth coat, the serene expression — the lot. What was even more remarkable was the other one, an absolute miniature Alsatian, complete with greyish tan legs and prick ears. His eyes depicted a state of armed neutrality, and the nose wrinkle showed he was memorising my scent.

It is a well known fact that you will always make a better dog if you can give him your individual attention as a youngster, but I wanted to be sure I kept the right one. I named them Steve and Roy and waited for them to sort themselves out. It did not take long, Steve rolled enthusiastically on a dead crow we fell in with, but Roy did not, although I invited him to. I also gave them each a piece of stick to carry, but sometimes Steve would lose his if his attention was diverted some way or another. The matter was therefore resolved. I sold Steve to Archie Shaw of Glencult in whose hands he gained quite a local reputation before he contracted hard pad and joined the majority. I concentrated as much as I could on trying to put the young Roy in the same league as his grandsire for he was developing into a magnificent specimen. He was to dogs as Muhammed Ali was to humans; the very make of him radiated power and speed superbly blended, whilst his quick understanding of new orders pro-

Roy at work with his sheep

ved he had it up top as well. The difference that stood out between him and old Ben was in their attitude to humans. While Ben loved being praised or clapped, Roy never in his life either asked for or wanted such flippancies. When you told him he was a grand chap for something he would just stand and look at you and say: "I know; what will we do now?" His repertoire was a bit more limited than Ben's; he would not turn troughs, and only brought a walking stick with a grudge, but he joined the élite after I had him photographed filling a barrow with turnips. So far as I know no other dog has undertaken this job, and people used to come to see him do it. The second best thing he liked doing was fighting — he was far too good at it and although I did not allow him to do it, I am sure that he had some way of getting another dog to assault him, and then thrashing him and claiming it was self defence.

He was what would be called in the outback a mean hombre; he got so that he would not let me belt him, and as he was so strong that I could not hold him except with both hands, he often got off with a shaking instead of a hammering. You could not keep a collar on him because his neck was bigger than his head. To take full advantage of this side of his character I taught him to arrest and hold humans as well as animals, and for some reason that I cannot recall, the command for that was: "He says you are hairy". This took him on the instant to the person indicated, where with teeth bared and birse up he challenged his charge to move or hardly breathe. Nobody ever tried to find out if he was bluffing. Roy was past his best but he developed great wisdom in the way he adapted himself to handling sheep on the rocky heights of Mount Blair, where every wrong move meant one over the rocks or a breakback by some cunning old bitch with three fleeces on to lie up in a bracken bed until dark. He had me beat both for sight and smell, but if I left him alone to get on with a gather, you seldom saw a beast left on his bit. Roy, probably as a result of the life he led, slowed up at about ten years of age, so I gave him to Ruth Dundas of Kinnaneil where he helped with the stirks and crossed ewes, slept on an electric blanket in the porch and enjoyed every luxury that his devoted mistress could keep him in. Like his illustrious relative Nell at Skirling Craig he was killed in the close by a lorry, this time a grain one. The best of Roy's kind are to be found on Dryburns and Chamberwells and of course Charlie Campbell's white one.

The next dog I had that deserves mention is Hector. With the different farms I was now handling I kept two dogs to cut down the chance of being left flat in the event of an accident. Hector was bred by George Coyne, a member of a famous herding family in Angus for some generations. All his life Geordie had good dogs, noted for endurance on wide hill ground, and he kept telling me about this time that he felt he had the best one up to date. He was to line one of his neighbour's bitches with him — he liked her and he wanted me to take the one that he would have got, so that in time he could get one back from me off him with some of old Ben's blood in his mother. He phoned one night to come up and get the pup; I did so and we had a beer in a hotel in Aberfeldy. Geordie said the pup was just like his father and he was sure to please me. They are one-manners, he said, and strangers cannot take liberties with them. That was the last time I saw Geordie. He and I both started herding on the Hatton in 1931, our first job from school, and stayed friends ever since. His swinging step devoured the hillside at a speed that few could match and none excel. He died of a heart attack within a year of giving me Hector. Hector was beautifully marked, pure black and white, his big white neck invaluable for seeing him at a distance on heather and his black equally effective on snow. As expected from his kind, distance was no object, the bigger the hill the better he liked it, he was a great gathering dog with loads of power yet safe with his mouth on animals. If the same could have been said about people I suppose I would have him yet.

He lived for one thing only — work — he would not carry a damned thing or associate himself with any activity except handling animals, with a marked preference for sheep. He was for some reason unable to punish cattle after he turned them; he refused to heel them so they just kept birling round in circles with the silly rascal hanging on to their ears, or nose. Another fault he had was that he could not stand a strange sheep being added to a flock; he was always shedding it off and standing it up against a fence. If you put him in charge of a beast and said "Keep that" he would have kept it standing till both died of hunger. Unfortunately he extended his enthusiasm in this habit to humans and started classifying visitors as acceptable or otherwise. He developed a particular dislike of children of a family on a neighbouring farm and I had to discipline him for threatening them when they came to see our children. One forenoon when I was in at the phone I heard a clatter followed by a child's screams outside and rushed out to find him standing over the girl concerned, having knocked her first off her bicycle. He was saved by the tearful intervention of both my own children and little Jane who was screaming that he had not bitten her sore. I advertised him as dangerous to children. Bill Mathers said he had no children where he stayed and gave me £80 for him. He has him still and boasts about his ability. I have stopped by a time or two if I see him going about the steading, but if he knows me he does not let on about it. I think he knows me all right and that is his way of retaliation for me selling him.

Once again I was flat on my tod so I got on the phone to John Edgar to get back to the old Ben and Nell kind. Next Sunday the Edgar family turned up with two pups off Craig, John's favourite son of Nell. Their mother Pat was brought over from Ireland by Ben to be his personal dog shortly before he died, and she had landed at the Craig. John had not a great deal of good to say about her and he would keep one off Craig and his own sister Nicky from the next litter for they were the right kind. There was one thing about Pat though; John said he had never seen her equal at the rear of a cattlebeast. "She can bite them every time their feet touch the ground, and after the first bite it's a fair distance before they land," he said. My cattle were badly in need of tuition as three years of Hector had them so that they would not move.

"Could you spare her for a few weeks till I get the pups going," I said, "I'll promise her a good time."

I took her off the train next day and after a day or two to make sure that she would not leave me, found an excuse to shift a field of sucklers. John was not joking; every cow that came at her got the treatment, first the nose and then not the heel, but the inside of the leg at the udder. The frantic bellows of the victims lifted the crows from the grain fields in excited cawing swarms, and in an hour the herd was as easily handled as the same number of low ground gimmers that had been used for a fortnight's practice for a trial. As John also said she was very ordinary at most other things, so I sent her back as soon as her son Steve began to work. Although he bore a resemblance to old Ben, he grew very much like his sire Craig. Almost as powerful as Roy, he was handicapped by a deformed forefoot, which he only put down in emergencies. Absolutely fearless and oblivious to pain he only gave a beast one chance to shift. As long as they were coming it was fine, but if one turned round to face him that was it. Once he charged, he would not stop and some part of the victim's anatomy was left dangling, and that is if it was lucky. More than one Border Leicester ewe suffered the loss of an ear; he caused the cows to take staggers by looking at them; he guarded me as his own personal property and no doubt would have had to be put down for an attack on somebody had I not killed him by accident by running over him with a bogey load of turnips which he was lying underneath guarding in case someone tried to take one. In a way I was glad; it would not have been easy to shoot him, he was some dog.

Having given his sister to my shepherd, here I was again — so on the phone once more. This time I drew a blank, John had sold Pat, lent Nicky out to a pal for the lambing, her pups were just newly speaned and all he was left with was Craig, who he said was in the bad books at the moment. One of his habits is to let any visiting stranger approach the door and knock. If an Edgar is at home and answers, all is well and Craig will resume his post underneath a barrow in the cartshed. The trouble is if nobody is at home, when the unlucky visitor is refused permission to go away. So long as he stands relatively still all is well, but it appeared that on this occasion the unlucky fellow, a packman, had attempted to depart. Depart he did, but without the seat of his pants and bits of his rump as well, leaving his bicycle propped against the wall. The contents of his case, which had burst open when he threw it away so he could run faster, were scattered round the close by a brisk east wind. I said to John, "You will have to put up a notice 'Beware of the Dog.' " "No, no," says John, "the news soon gets round folk like that: we were home at four, he could have sat down on the summer seat and waited."

Since John could not help me I gave John McMillan a phone and told him my predicament. John always has about twenty about him, as that is one of his ways of making a living. I went away up to get one and got my usual kind reception from the family for whom I have the greatest admiration. Beatrice is a topper — miles from anywhere, she scrubs her pretty daughters, helps John on the farm and generally answers the description of what a farmer's wife should be. Whether I was too fussy I do not know, but I was always looking for something better than John was letting me see and told him so.

"The only dog you haven't seen working is Craig," he said, "My stud dog and he is not for sale."

"Let's have a look, John," I said. "Seeing him won't do any harm."

This was a different story — here was a dog worth having. Both his good bitches were in whelp to him, but I could not wait for them. I left with Craig on loan till I got something and we got fond of him. He was a topper with sheep but had never been used on cattle, and he intended to keep it that way. If you sent him for them he pretended they did not exist and just kept going until he got sheep. That was his only snag, he was friendly to everybody, clean in his habits and a pleasure to work. My family urged me to buy him or send him back in case anything happened to him, and as I saw John had bought another big priced one at an auction, I phoned him up and agreed a price — with John retaining the stud rights. I sent him ten pounds more than we said to get something for the bairns. About a fortnight later he brought down a bitch for him, but also one of Callag's pups from Craig's first litter.

"That's your luckpenny," said John, "He's ten weeks old, registered and working the hens already. If you tell me what you are to call him I'll phone the Society and they will send you his card."

I looked at the morsel at my feet, one lug sticking up and the other down — the very image of Basil Brush. The thought was tempting, but I resisted, "Tell you what, John, we'll name him Fred."

I had just heard about the incident in the stable, when one of the three wise men who had come to adore the infant stood on a besom that had been left lying on the floor, when the shaft sprung up and hit him on the face, the pain of which blow drew from him the ex-clamation "Jesus Christ!" "My goodness," said Joseph, "That's a good name; we were going to name him Fred."

Anyway, after the ritual examination for ticks and vermin of any kind which my womenfolk put pups through, and thoroughly bath-ed and washed with Lifebuoy soap, the scruffy looking little mer-chant joined the team.

John was right about the hens; our ducks got the treatment right away and were marched backwards and forwards round the steading whenever opportunity occurred. Nor was taking to the dam an escape, the bold boy swam after them with the one lug sticking up as usual. I used to think that he was the ugliest pup I had had, but you had to like him for the kind way he treated everything. It was at this time of my life that something went wrong with my knees and I was so taken up with trying to get them better that I did not spend enough time teaching him to retrieve like Roy or Ben, so the fact that he does not carry is my blame, not his. His pups are naturals. One thing soon became clear, he was a better one than his father, equal in all respects at sheep and able on cattle as well. One confrontation with a cattle beast is enough, and then it is on its way with Fred swinging on its tail in ecstasy. It is queer how they never kick when this happens, but it is not because they like it if one is to go by the howls.

When Fred was about a year old it dawned on me that I had another one way out. I noticed that he had changed. The lug had come down and was like its neighbour, the dirty brown colour of his tan had changed to deep deep red, his black was black, and his white shining. His brow had widened and muscles bulged in all the right places. His work was polished and decisive and he joined the children at all their games with boisterous enthusiasm. It was about this time that he developed his love of a swing. Sally had a rope tied to the branch of a beech tree in the garden and he started leaping up and hanging on to it. By adjusting the height she soon had him suspended about a foot off the ground when she would pile him like a ten year old piles her little sister, to the joyous gurgles of the delighted Fred. In no time he began to be able to do it on his own, and if you came out of the house in the evening that was where you were most likely to find him. To give him every chance of making the charts he had to get as much work as I could give him so I asked John McMillan for permission to sell his father. I got it and Craig is now on Daldorn with Tom McGregor, and very highly regarded both as a worker and a breeder, while Fred is lying beside me as I write. I suppose he is a bit unlucky that I got him when I was 59 instead of 29, but of all the dogs I have owned he is the most suited to be an old man's dog because of his ability to interest himself in harmless pursuits instead of getting into mischief. If I am working with a tractor on Bridgend, Fred's job is to prevent the seagulls and crows from landing so he has some very busy days at seed time. He will also spend an afternoon digging out a rabbit or an hour persuading me to shift a bag of beet pulp to allow him to get the mouse that is under it. He also loves to catch drips of water falling from a rhone pipe, or tracking foxes. It was only when the snow revealed the identity of the visitor that I understood why he always took the identical way along a certain area of steep and rough ground. His nose is superb; he tells me which burrows to gas for rabbits and I have yet to find him in error. I have brought him back to a hole that I thought was inhabited and which he said was not, and he thinks he is insulted, but you can hardly shift him from one that he says is, until it has been gassed and sealed. One of his best points is his ability to hold sheep round me in a bucht for dosing or innoculation, for it gives me the use of both hands instead of having to use one to hold the beast with. Another useful aspect from an old man's point of view is the no effort catching system. I tell him the beast I want, then go and stand in the nearest corner, leaving one sheep width between myself and the fence. Fred duly arrives with his charge which seeks refuge in the apparent shelter and I just put down my hand.

I was letting Will Rennie of Berryhill, Kelso, see him at some of his stuff. Willie is au fait with all the things and people in the farming world but especially keen on dogs.

"Willie," I said at the end, "Is that the best dog you have ever seen?"

Willie thought long and hard and I could visualise all the dogs that were passing through his brain. At last he spoke.

"Well Jim, I'm no to gang as far as that, but there's one thing I will say, I never saw a better one."

Willie had been out last year with some collies to Finland and had stayed to teach the Finns how to work them. The exporter would have liked Fred, as a really outstanding specimen to upgrade the native strain, but he is getting on fine where he is. He is under tuition just now from Sally for his higher English, responding by growl or whine, or tail wagging to the various phrases uttered in absolute monotone. The passage she uses is from Old Tam Dorat's instructions to the teenage Kirriemarians over 100 years ago on how to 'pan' a dog. "Anybody can pan a dog, min, it's the startin o' him that counts — the root o' the tail in ae hand min, the cuff o' the neck in the ither, point him the way you want him to gang — a fung on the erse — and doon the road he'll go min, just like a locomotive min, just like a locomotive.'' When it comes to — ''the root'' Fred bares his teeth in disapproval of the action, but at ''a fung on the erse'' he snaps viciously at his tormentor in a display of mock anger so realistic that I call a halt to the game in case he is not joking. The phrase ''a fung on the erse'' is to Fred what ''He says you are hairy'' was to Roy.

I won't go on about him any longer other than to mention one more good point. He will go with anybody that I tell him to, to help for a busy day, and if he hears a handling going on on the neighbouring farm he will ask me if he can go and help, though I never let him in case he is not wanted. If I am at the market I give him to the chap in charge of the sheep pens and there is nothing the two of them enjoy better than droving and shedding ready for the grader. He takes hares on the run in about the same proportion as those that get away, but I fear now that he is nearly five that the odds in favour of the hare will lengthen.

There have been four litters off him but I will only mention one of them. My ex-grieve Joe Troup is now manager of the neighbouring estate and purchased a pure black bitch to enable him to help with the animals. She had a difficult job, as Joe had no idea of how to work her and the two of them had to start at the beginning. However, with mutual patience and sometimes without it, they struggled away and gradually began to get the better of things. I encouraged Joe to treat her well, for she had a lot to put up with, and soon he was showing her off to me standing beside him on the tractor seat looking out through the windscreen. I finally decided she was good enough to be the mother of Fred's pups, for which I had had some enquiries, so I offered Joe eight pounds each for every pup she had at 8 weeks. She had ten one very frosty night, but three were dead before morning. I took the survivors and got in touch with my customers, I sold six, three dogs, three bitches, and was left with a little chap that I called Ernest because of the way he followed every move I made. He was bare skinned and prick-eared, beautifully marked and as handsome at his age as his dad had been plain. Nor was this all, he worked from the first sheep he saw, he copied his father in everything he did and me in everything he could. He carried anything he could lift, he turned over divots when we were looking for worms, he gathered stones beside me and he had my slippers ready before I got my boots off. I have a habit of chewing a stalk of cocksfoot grass at certain times of the year, so I had to pull one for him to chew as well and people stopped to see the two of us walking up the road side by side with the grass sticking out of the corner of our mouths.

Alas, with all the other commitments I now have I felt it was unfair to both him and his father to keep them both, and as Sally would not hear of selling Fred I advertised him at eight months old fully broken, cattle or sheep, carry to gun. I put a price on him that would guarantee that whoever bought him would be good to him. John McMillan phoned, came down and bought him to be his stud dog at Balhomish but he said to me later that he had got an offer from America he was finding hard to refuse. So Ernie, my little pal, wherever you are, I wish you well, and I hope your owner appreciates you. As Willie Walker of Crammie said to him one evening when they were passing the time of day. "By God, Ernie, you are some boy."

While on the subject of Willie Walker, all 6' 3" of him, his father went to Newtyle School with me, and his aunt Mary was a very pretty school girl. Will was on the phone the other night asking how I was keeping. It was not long before we were on the dogs and the animals and I asked how his dog was doing. I had seen him work a time or two, and thought he could use a few more brains.

"Ach," Will says, "he's working awa, in fact Annie (his wife) was saying the last day that she was sure he could be better if I was more friendly to him, and I think there's maybe something in what she says. I don't suppose he is too bad as a dog but I just don't like him as a person."

To people who understand, that sentence says it all. Will is a sort of grown up Graham Walls, he has retained the wisdom and vision only available to those who live in remote places. I like him a lot.

Here is another story about dogs. Some twenty years ago I accepted an invitation to address the annual dinner of the West Perthshire Sheep Dog Association at Callendar, so I thought I would make the most of it. I took Roy and my herd early to the hall and hid both in an anteroom with instructions to Dougal to let Roy out when I whistled. It was a very rainy night but a company of 140 had gathered for the occasion. I bemoaned the fact that the dogs of today were brainless compared to those of long ago and instanced Hoggs Hector who, if he heard his master say he was going somewhere the following day, would sneak off on his own and be waiting at the said place when his master turned up. "Compare the idiot that I have the bad luck to own. This afternoon on the hill I was urging him to hurry — 'do you no ken you muckle lump that I have to be at Callendar tonight at half past seven.' When I went to shut him up before I came away he was nowhere to be found and has not been found yet so far as I know, although I whistled for him like this for about a minute: 'Whee' ". Through the lobby and right up to my chair trotted the big fellow and in mock amazement

I said "Well, I'll be damned." Everyone sat quiet, then one chap said out loud, "I don't believe it — he's no even wet."

Last year I paid a return visit in the same capacity to the same association, but there was one table at the far away end of the hall where some had had too much to drink and would not keep quiet when I was speaking, so I closed my notes and told them that manners, like dogs, had deteriorated over the last few years, and to ask me back when theirs were mended. Tom McGregor was the chairman. I stayed the night with him and his charming wife, had a wonderful time and saw Craig working in the morning.

Today is the 1st of January 1983. Sal is 20 and was out on the town last night till 5 o'clock in the morning. She has a young man who comes in to our house. I get on well with him, he has good literary sense and I thought I would try out one of my stories on him to get his reaction. I gave him "The Wall Boy" and he dutifully said it was great. "Seven for over a year," he gurgled, "That's really something." While we were discussing how to get these stories into print, Fred was as usual on the job, and Sal said, "What a good dog, I see you have brought your ball." I wondered what I had written about the big rascal, now over seven years old and still behaving like a pup, so I had a check. I note that I had said that I had forgotten to teach him to carry and that was true, but time has passed since I wrote about him, and in fairness to the dog I have to add to this chapter.

On the 14 November 1979 I had a letter from the Prime Minister saying she intended to recommend me to the Queen as being suitable for an OBE if I had no objections, and needless to say I replied by return in case she changed her mind. I had not been feeling well for some time; I was too easily tired and got aches in my gums when carrying bales up hills. I was on the point of going to Fin McKenzie to see what was wrong when I got Mrs. Thatcher's letter and I thought: "I'll keep quiet about myself until I get my award." In due course it was published and I had about a week answering all the letters of congratulation — nearly 100, some from ex-students abroad, some from people I had not met since the war; my heart was full, and my cup running over. As my physical condition was not improving I was just on the point of going to Dr McKenzie when I got another letter, asking if I would come down to Buckingham Palace on the 4th February to get my medal from Her Majesty. Although I had some misgivings I again put off my examination, for I thought Fin might not let me go. Complete with wife and two daughters I travelled to London and had a wonderful two days, when of course I was privileged to get my medal from the Queen, in a scene of pageantry and splendour surrounded by the treasures of the world collected from all parts of the earth and stored in the

The Author and his Wife 1969

residence of the Queen — even as the bees store their gathered treasure. Coming home when we arrived at Dundee I carried two big suitcases over the flyover steps, and I never felt anything so heavy. I could not keep up with the women, the sweat was soaking my shirt and I wondered if I was going to make it. I did though and even drove home, though Nan said I was driving badly. Next day I did go to Finlay McKenzie and he took my blood pressure.

"Your journey was necessary," said Fin, "Your blood pressure is far too high. I will give you some tablets, but I want you to come back on Friday for a cardiograph, and don't do anything daft in the interval, like lifting cars out of ditches in snowstorms." I had managed to get Fin's car out of a ditch on the Meams brae the year before.

On Friday I presented myself for the cardiograph. The nurse that was to do it was Irene McVittie, pretty as a picture smelling as usual like honeysuckle, and I was lying looking at her assembling her machine thinking how lucky we were in Angus to have girls like her taping little wires onto one's legs and chest. However in no time we were set and she switched on the machine. The tape came out with its graph and after a while she stopped it.

"I've been thinking this thing must be needing serviced for a while now," she said, "It cannot be like that."

She checked all the connections and tried again.

"Just lie still," she said, "I want Dr McKenzie to have a look at this."

Dr McKenzie studied the tape, "Tell you what, Jim," he said, casual like, "I want you to go home guietly and go to your bed till I get a friend of mine to examine you — this is not what it should be. I'll try and get him out tomorrow." Wondering what was up I obeyed but was no sooner in bed than he phoned.

"I've been having another look at that tape," he said, "and I have phoned McLean to come out right now."

Sure enough, before an hour was up, the two of them turned up and the specialist got going with his machines.

"Well, Finlay," he said when he had finished, "You are right enough, Mr. Findlay has suffered a heart attack some days ago, but we seem to have got him in time, and if he behaves, there is no reason why he should not recover. He must rest completely for eleven weeks to enable the heart to recover its efficiency, in bed for four weeks, not out of the house for the next four, and three weeks before he gets back to the farm. By the way, Mr Findlay, for the rest of your life you will have to operate to the following rule — before you do anything, look at it and decide whether it is to be easy or difficult; if it's easy, do it, if it isn't, don't." I have lived by that maxim ever since, and I mean to keep it that way.

The days were long lying in bed feeling like a broken down baler waiting for a part to come from Kilmarnock, and though Nan had plenty volunteers to help with the sheep and Fred was out with her morning and afternoon, he had taken up residence at the side of my bed, and by many a nudge with the nose if one of my arms was above the blankets let me understand he was needing me up and out. Having had no luck that way, you may imagine my feelings when the big chap arrived in my room one day carrying one of my boots which he laid down at the side of the bed. "What a good boy for fetching it" I said in ecstasy, and made much of him, telling him he was now by far better than Ernie or Roy or even Ben. I got up, put on the boot, and walked about the house with him, even though the four weeks were not quite up. He was nearly six years old at the time and from that day he has carried on command, and such is his strength that I have got him to jump over a four foot rabbit-netted fence, carrying a full grown hare. Willie Rennie was up last summer as usual, and I told him to select any ewe in a field of 70 and I would get Fred to bring her right up to the gate without us going into the field. In a few minutes the job was done and Fred was lying keeping his charge at the gate, when a car stopped. It was Jim and Cath Lindsay, now from Dun, having a run round their old district. Willie could not contain himself although he did not know the Lindsays. "I've just seen a thing I would not have believed," he said. "That dog brought that ewe out among the rest and up to the gate himself and it was the one I picked; by God, I tell you it's hardly believable." Jim got out of his car to get a better look. "There's nothing strange about that, Mister," he said, "That's Fred."

Jim Pearson has two good bitches, Nanny and Jess, and both are in whelp to him just now. Jess is a grand-daughter of Jock Richardson's famous Wiston Cap.

Jim Coates, the Kinpurnie Keeper of the 30's, was another that could move on a hill. He used to tie poachers to trees till he had time to collect them, and said he could not understand any gamekeeper who kept a cat. "There's one thing about cats and partridges," he said, "and that is that they won't agree." Although I have said elsewhere that the dog will mould himself to some extend on his master, there are millions of us whose dog's personality is more dominant than ours, to whom our good points are no use because we have subconsciously been graded as inferior, and unfit to copy. There are many other examples. If you bring up a lamb on a goat, you can watch it run the top of a dyke, or stand on top of a garden shed years after it has last seen its foster mother — it has adopted her personality and accepted her ways. Conversely I know a red setter that dominates the family of six humans that belong to him. He is the one who decides when the family go to bed at night and rise in the morning, which way he exercises them on the lead, and when it is time to come in from the garden. He does not like me, because he knows what would happen if he was teamed up with me, although I have only advised him verbally to stay away from my property. If I keep on about dogs, I will not be able to speak about cattle or sheep or soldiers or shepherds, but I have seen the blur that was Moss running the face of Troloss, and Nap walking in a straight line through a fence 100 yards away although the gate was open three feet away. I have seen Roy bring in a straggler off nearly the top of Mount Blair, and the other Troloss Moss — him of the short tail — charge the £600 Weston Cupwinner like an express train leaving both tup and dog bleeding like stuck pigs.

"In the name of God, Ben," I said "you've killed them both."

"Maybe so," said Ben, "but when I tell Stump to come on, that's what he does."

It is at least 4,000 years since men and dogs first discovered the mutual benefits to be gained by teaming up together. It may be 20,000 for all I know, but I base my figure at 4,000 because the Pharoahs hunted with them in their lifetime and were guarded by them after death in the God-inhabited body of Anubis. I am sure that if Bill had written as much about humans as I have now written about dogs, his friend and master would have praised him like this:

"Splendid altogether, William, but you've done fine noo and you must be dry; I think you should run down to the burn for a drink."

HOW FAR BACK DOES ONE GO?

The Egyptian theologists believed that the cycle of a soul was 3,000 years, 1,000 in the human form, 1,000 in the animal and likewise in the bird. Now I do not want readers to wager large sums of money on the strength of my having said it was the Egyptians. It was actually, but it would not have mattered if it had been the Greeks or the Hindus, although I would not put too much credibility on it had it been the Celts or the Incas, in spite of the insistence of the last named that everything happened in tens.

I have decided however, that things occur in our physical lifetime that cannot be explained by Pythagorus, Newton, Marconi and that lot, so some outside or — if it is the soul — inside influence is also at work somewhere. If the lifespan is 70 years and everybody got a fair go and the soul has its 1,000 years to go it could only do fourteen people and 20 years of the last one, who would have to soldier on for his next 50 without a soul to guide him. This is the reason we do not all die at the same age.

There have been an instance or two in my own life so far that have remained a mystery, and that will not be erased from my memory. The first happened when I was about five. I had got a present of a real policeman's whistle from my doting grand-mother. It was an expensive gift (half a crown), if memory serves, and in 1920 that was money. When I got home I got earnest instructions from my mother to look after it and on no account to lose it like most of the other toys I had had. So, threading a bit of thick white string through the ring on the end, I hung it round my neck and set out to acquaint anything that could hear of my good fortune. Its piercing blast sent the kittens scurrying underneath the pile of brushwood left over from bedding the stacks, while the sparrows flew from the heads of the unthatched one that had been tirred for an early morning thresh next day, and took cover in the safety of the Scotch firs behind the farmhouse. The miller's big roan cow and her yearling stirk came looking over the top of the fence to see what the racket was about, but there was no sign of what I wanted — the cottar bairns coming out to the jealous and asking for a shottie. I thought the five year old equivalent of "Ach well, Mohammed had to go to the mountain" and set off along the footpath that ran alongside the lade and which led to the cottar houses in which dwelt various small Reids, Wildgooses, and Dallases. I looked forward to turning their visages green on witnessing my new possession, from which I continued to emit blasts which would have done justice to a French Rugby referee attempting to get a Welsh scrum-half to desist from standing with both feet on the face of a prostrate English prop-forward. Probably as a result of the racket a water hen emerged from some brushwood, and made off towards the safety of the Noran with that slightly ungainly walk common to all birds more at home on water than on land. Wondering what she had been up to and if her mate was still among the broom, I clambered up the bank using both hands to assist me. After a search of the area revealed nothing, I jumped down from the top of the bank on to the path, landing on all fours to lessen the impact on my feet. At the time I did not know that that was the reason for landing that way; a child does it naturally, like a cat. I was made aware of the scientific advantages of the position some twenty years later by the Army instructors on unarmed combat. When I resumed my normal perpendicular position I noticed that my whistle was lying where I had landed but that its string was still round my neck. Not only that, the knot was still secure, and I had to pull it over my head to get it off. I examined the whistle to see if there was a gap in the ring where the string could have got out, but no, not even a crack. I sat down on the bank and tried every way I could think of to get the whistle back on to the string without undoing the knot and was beat. Because the knot was tight I had to take it to my mother who cut it with the gully (that is what bread knives are called in rural areas), put the whistle back on and told me not to take it off again. This time it stayed on, and finally took its place (complete with string) in the big drawer at the bottom of the chest, where superseded toys awaited the arrival of a new child in the family. More than forty-five years later the memory of that whistle flooded back to me as I stood and looked at a sneck an inch away from its staple that had been the right length the day before.

It was in the first gate of the sheep buchts on Aucharroch. This is always left open at the end of a handling so as not to lose the impetus of the run up next time we wanted sheep in. This morning when I drew round the gate behind the now penned flock I could not engage the sneck and just thought that somebody had shifted either sneck or staple. It was impossible that the staple had been moved, for on examination it was right on the near edge of the post, so I thought it was the sneck, and went for a set of tools to put it back where it belonged. It hung from a staple driven through one of the bars of the gate about eighteen inches along, to give added strength to the gate to take the back pressure of sheep unwilling to proceed up the system. I drove the staple in a bit so that I could lever straight the ends which had been clenched and then I realised that it had not been previously moved. The spar showed no telltale hole of any previous position. I laid everything down and lit a cigarette to help me think and to rot my lungs (although the second effect was not intentional), and tried to find the answer but there wasn't one. The gate hung on a post at the end of a five rail fence which post could neither turn nor lean. At the other end the post was secured to a cemented wall as straight and plumb as it was the day before. Neither the shepherd nor the grieve could offer any explanation, and neither thought much about it.

"Standing looking at it'll no sort it," said Joe, the grieve, "If there is nothing else you are needing me for, I want away to the silage." He was right enough so I levered out the sneck, and shifted the staple about an inch along the 4' x 2", where it has operated efficiently ever since. The memory of the whistle flooded back. I saw again my mother sawing away at the string with her gully — she used her left hand for everything but writing. That is another queer thing, although I am right handed, if I ever take up cricket or golf, I will need clubs for a leftie. Maybe the same bat will do; I will need advice on that.

I think there is a lot to be said for the way things are. As a child you admit your inability to understand, but you are confident that you will when you are big. When you are in your prime you dismiss the things you do not understand as unimportant and trivial hiccups in the panorama of your all-embracing intellect. When you get old enough to look back you wonder if somewhere along the way of the evolution of mankind, the soul has forgotten to feed some factor into the computerised automatic understanding department, leaving us spinning in a world where we can get all of the answers some of the time or some of the answers all of the time, but never all of the answers all of the time.

THE WALL BOY

The grieve on the neighbouring farm to Bridgend of Balloch (doesn't that name tug at the heartstrings?) was called Ally Walls. He lived in the farmhouse with his wife and two children, Angela and Graham. Angela was 10 and Graham 7, and they were bussed the five miles daily to Kingoldrum School. They were at that time of their lives absolutely innocent of sophistication of any sort whatever, already wise in the ways of nature, bursting with healthy energy and inquisitiveness. They were in fact what is now called completely uninhibited. Mounted bareback on their ponies, Angela's a huge garron named Slater, and Graham's an elderly Dartmoor type mare called Cherry, and with only a halter on their heads, the children could control their mounts to any speed on any ground in a way that convinced me of the authenticity of the way that Indian braves are depicted charging the wagon train in the westerns. Slater was a one girl horse and would not suffer himself to be caught by other than his mistress. He even played a game with her, rushing up in a truly menacing attitude, and pretending he was to savage her, but he stopped at the last minute, was scolded for his bad manners, cuddled and rewarded with a crust of bread. It was indeed an inspiring sight on a summer's evening to see the two tiny riders silhouetted against Catlaw, galloping forth on an after-school inspection of the farm. As most of our work on our farm is done in the evenings, we were invariably visited by the pair. Angela would sit on Slater and chatter away, but Graham always had to be helping, and his non-stop conversation continually produced gems of innocence and originality.

One night when Nan, Sally and I were burning brushwood, Graham was relating the important things of the day.

"Fell down out of a tree the night," he said "I was up at the tap of it tae and I wisna greetin."

"By Jove, Graham," I said, "You are a tough one, there's very few loons that widna greet if they fell out of the top of a tree."

"That's right," said Graham, "I am a tough one."

His sister was not impressed; from her lofty pedestal on Slater's withers she observed: "Stop blawing, you're feart of Slater anyway."

"I'm no the only one," said Graham, "Stallions are dangerous."

"Blethering little — " said Angela, "Slater's no a stallion — he's cut."

"I didna say he wasna cut, he's been cut for the last fourteen years, I said he was a stallion," said the wee fellow. Angela, with the superior knowledge of her ten years looked at him pitingly and then at us as much as to say "some sisters have them".

I have a compelling urge to gather stones off all kinds of land, and this Saturday Graham and I were carting them off a newly sown barley field. Seeing my assistant approaching clutching a stone against his tummy of about the same weight as himself, I remonstrated. "Graham, you pick up the little ones that you can manage," I said, "That's far too big a stone for a boy of six to carry." He dropped it at once so he could get breath to put me right. "Six," he said, "I'm no six, I'm seven — I've been seven for over a year." Not half an hour later we met one that was too heavy for me to lift on to the bogey, so I took Fergie Gray to reduce it to liftable proportions. Fergie is the name of the great hammer given to me on his retirement by its owner. He used it in the family quarry after he had lost his left forearm in stone breaking machinery, with the help of his stump he raised it as high as he could, then let it fall on the selected boulder.

At my best, no stone could withstand Fergie's onslaught, but of late either he or I have mellowed, and with mechanical diggers practically on every farm to bury sitfasts on site, hammers like Fergie and people like me are becoming out of date. Anyway, having assured the stone there was nothing to worry about — winking to Graham at the same time and asking him to stand back in case of splinters, I smote with all I had, and split it right through the middle, exposing a circular pattern of darker colour. (I built this stone side by side into the west bank of the Quharity to secure the bank against erosion, where I hope it will be seen from now on). Graham's mouth was wide open but he concealed his disbelief.

"How heavy are you?" he said as casually as he could.

"Well, Graham, I admit I am too heavy; the last time I weighed myself I was sixteen stone."

"Is that so?" said Graham, "my mother is twenty-two stone."

"Do you tell me that, Graham; that's a great weight for a woman, I must have a right look at her sometime. She must be quite big to be that weight."

"Not really," said Graham, "she's no a that big, round about ten feet."

We changed the subject, but I could not get the lady out of my mind. About a week later when the two of us were looking at the lambs I could resist no longer. "Graham," said I, "Since you told me about your mother I've often thought about her. How is she getting on?''

"She is getting on fine, though she dented the car yesterday" said he. "She is on a diet."

"You don't say," I replied, "is it working?"

"Aye," said he, "It's working grand, she is putting on weight."

Another day we were fencing and Graham was holding the wire in the right position for the staple when he presented his little hands up in front of me. "What do you think of these for a pair of hands?" I wanted so much to say the right thing.

"As good a pair of hands as ever I have seen on a chap your age," I tried, "What do you think of them yourself?"

"Full of energy" was the answer as he grabbed the wire at the next post.

"That's your tongue you are talking about" observed Angela, seated as usual on her obedient Slater.

Two years ago the farm changed hands and the Walls moved to Craigeassie where Dad is now grieve. Cherry reverted to her original owner Jim Lindsay now at Leys of Dun, and Slater was sold for £180 at the farm roup. He was ridden into the sale ring by a tearful Angela, and I stood like some dummy and witnessed the tragedy. Thousands of times since when I picture the two of them, the huge and powerful pony whose only thought was to obey the will of a slip of a girl, and her absolute assurance that this situation was normal and an everyday occurrence, I have regretted not buying him and giving him to her. By this time secondary education will be whittling away at the spontaneous wisdom and instinctive values of my two little pals. The pressures of our times will engulf them like the rest of us; we can none of us re-arrange society or put back the clock. A few of us are privileged to behold and to cherish scenes such as I have just related. Long may the hills and remote places continue to produce people like Angela and Graham, for of such is the life-blood of the nation.

THE CROWN OF THORNS

It was a rough kind of night in March 1956 and it had been a rough kind of day as well for my mother had taken some kind of turn and was blacking out periodically. The doctor had done all he could and we had to keep her in bed and give her anything she wanted. I had been up twice during the day. She lived with my sister in a big house only one mile away, but as the ewes were lambing I had to be with them. I had settled down for the night in the cartshed beside the ewes when Nan came and said I was wanted up at Couston — a specialist had been called who had advised my sister that mother could not last till morning. They had discussed the possibility of taking her to Dundee for treatment by some special heart machine, but the professor had said she would not survive the journey, and she would be better to pass away where she was. When I got to her room, everybody was sitting quietly but they went out when I came in. She was lying on her back as if asleep, and her right arm folded across the blanket above her breast. I took her hand in mine and bent down so my mouth was just beside her ear and said, "What's going on, C.D.?" Her initials were Charlotte Duncan and C.D. was my pet name for her. She opened her eyes and looked at me. Her eyes were very blue and she said, "Jim, what are you doing back here — you've been up twice today — why are you not watching the ewes?"

I said, "Mum, the ewes don't matter when you are ill; I have lots of them, but I have only one of you."

"Well, well," she said, "it's good to be thought a lot of, but you could have come tomorrow in daylight surely."

I did not know what to say to that one, so I did not say anything. She lay looking at me — the bedside lamp was set in such a way that she was in the shade and I saw a startled look come onto her face.

"You're surely not thinking I am dying," she said, "with all these doctors and folk examining me?"

Again it wasn't easy but I had to try. "Well, Mum, to tell you the truth, the specialist thinks it would be too dangerous to try to take you to the hospital, and they told me to come up to see you just in case you got any worse."

"Ah" she said, "Now I see it all. Well, I can tell you I am not dying and I won't be dying for some years yet, after Alex has finished his education and is fit to earn his own living." (Alex was my sister's son, and mum looked after him when his mother was teaching).

"By jove, you are a tougher; if I was sure you were right I would get you into Dundee to get this new treatment to speed up your recovery."

"I am sure," she replied, "and if you need more convincing I will tell you how I am sure. When I was having that sleep before you wakened me I was dreaming and thinking about Alex, and Jesus came and stood beside me. After a while he said "Take up thy bed and walk,' and then he went away."

"That was a braw dream, Mum," I said, "but how are you sure it was Jesus?"

"Because his brow was all scratched and bleeding, where they had crowned him with the thorns."

The warmth of her conviction and the serenity that was always hers dispelled any doubt that was left. I went through to where the others were in the sitting room — it was quarter past eleven now. I said to all and sundry: "Phone for an ambulance, and get her into hospital." The heart specialist said, "If you say so, but I warn you she will not survive the journey."

Dr Sim picked up the phone and began to ask for the number. I said to Gordon Frew, "Would you like a bet?" Eight years later when Alex was set up in business and employing three men, Mum lost her appetite and we got her to go to Meigle hospital for a check up. All examinations were negative, but yet she would not eat and lost weight at an alarming rate. Again I had a crack about things with her, and asked for her explanation.

"Well, Jim, my work here is finished now and I'm wearied to get away to my ain folk. I hope you and Alex will look after Millicent when I'm away."

I did not like the way things were going so I tried to change the subject. I was standing in a Council election in a fortnight so I said, "I hope you will vote for me at the election anyway."

"No, Jim." She looked at me. "I nearly called you Gordon, I know you are my son, but I have been a Conservative all my life and I'll vote for Sir James Duncan." Sir James was our MP and a friend as well. "Now leave me, Gordon," she said, "I am needing a rest."

At her funeral less than a week later my emotion was hard to control. I do not think she would have approved. Mothers do have a powerful influence in their offspring's behaviour, but I think I can truthfully say that whatever bad things I have about me I did not get them from my mother.

HITCH YOUR WAGON TO A STAR

It was nearly or exactly the longest day of 1975. It had been as usual one of the big days of the agricultural year, the judging of the livestock at the Highland, with its triumphs and celebrations and its disappointments and celebrations, for no matter whether you win or lose you drink on the night of the judging, for you have been preparing your beasts for long weeks and months for this day — so now when it is over you let down your hair.

I had had a narrow escape. The judge of a breed that shall be nameless (but they are scarce of wool when they are lambed) was late, and the chief steward had almost bullied me into judging them when he turned up, so I had ample excuse to celebrate my good fortune. For reasons best known to themselves, the governers of the

East of Scotland College of Agriculture always invite me to their sherry party. It is a function which I take a special effort to attend, for I meet many of my fellow governers of the past and for an hour and a half we exchange memories of bygone board meetings and College conferences, and how if you grow potatoes on the same patch nine years in a row with no fertilizer application you can get them reduced to the size of robin's eggs with a dry matter content of 92, and which when immersed in boiling water immediately explode, causing heavy mortality amongst the flies who happen to be upside down on the ceiling at the time. Jackie Hughes, the college officer, knows that I feel embarrassed if I have an empty glass in my hand at a party of this kind and by the time that all but the reckless had departed there was not much room for blood in my alcohol stream.

Fortunately, having forseen this possibility I had arranged my timetable for getting home beforehand and by the back of 10 o'clock and several ham sandwiches later, I set off for Aucharroch. The roads were practically deserted and with the long stretch of dual carriageways I was in Perth just shortly after eleven. I was just on the Forfar side of Scone at Newmains Farm, the late tenant of which was Andrew Bryden who was tragically killed in a car accident and who had been a fellow governer for 17 years, when I observed a long thin person indicating he needed a lift. I work on the principle that it might be my turn some day, so I drew up alongside and opened the door. Sitting himself comfortably and shutting the door, rather harder than I would have advised, my passenger spoke thus.

"May the Lord bless you and keep you for picking me up this night."

I did not lower the standard. "He makes his face to shine upon me every day of my life — may he do to you likewise."

He said "Just as I am — I am" and lapsed into silence. I was not to let him off like that so I asked where he was making for, and he said Aberdeen. I had a guess at his age, I thought about 70, and I ventured the opinion that it was not usual for a chap at his time of life to be on an evening stroll of 88 miles and what would he have done if I had not picked him up.

"I would have walked until I dropped," he said "Or maybe got a lift from a fish lorry, but my pal is taking me to Orkney tomorrow and he is leaving at 9 o'clock. I spend a week in Orkney occasionally and this is my chance of getting there. I should never have come on this — he used a rude adjective — bus trip, and when I get back I will resign from the club that left me stranded in Perth. The organiser said we could do what we liked so long as we were back at the bus park at 9 o'clock, I am sure I was back in time, but the b— thing had left — as I said, the Lord must have sent you."

I accepted with some satisfaction this divine responsibility and wanted to know more. "I think I should know your name," I said, "there's no good me calling you Fred if your name is Tom, and what will your wife be thinking and you not on the bus?"

"Just call me Jimmie, and I'm no married," said he and then again, "Just as I am I am."

The mood got into me too, "There's no doubt about it," I said, "The Lord is your shepherd, and he has deputised me to get you home some way or other, so I'll tell you what I'll do. I'll sponsor you eight miles for every verse of the 23rd you can start — you sing the first line and I'll join you the rest of the verse."

The contented hum of the BMW seemed like the church organ setting the tune as Jimmie started. His voice was pleasant and we got through the verse really well. As the quiet waters by faded into silence I waited — but nothing came.

"Jimmie," I said, "you are not doing very well, that will only get you to Burrelton. Pray man, to those that ask shall be given."

He lifted up his voice triumphantly. "No matter where you are, Hitch your wagon to a star, Heaven can't be very far, From lovely Stornoway."

As we sang together, I was uplifted by his inspiration and it was infectious. "Jimmie, I'll give you sixteen miles for that one, plus an assist to get started the next two," I enthused, "You can take it you are the length of Brechin before I leave you."

We got through the rest happily and uneventfully before we reached Coupar Angus. "See these lights over there," said Jimmie pointing, "That's Alyth; there's a grand pub there called the Commercial. I canna mind the name of the folk that have it."

"Repper" said I.

"That's them all right," said he, "and those other lights farther away, that's Kirrie, the best pub there is the White Horse."

"By God, Jimmie," I said, "you know your pubs, what about Coupar Angus?"

"Oh that's the Railway Inn," quoth he, "Everybody knows that."

"There is another thing I know now, Jimmie," I said, "and that is the reason you missed the bus."

"No, no, I won't have that, the thing could have waited for me. I've waited plenty of times for folk the 23 years I drove buses round here," he insisted, "I never left anybody like I've been left today. This has put me off buses, but seeing I've lost my licence just now I suppose I'll just have to put up with them."

"You tell me you've lost your licence, Jimmie," I said, "Surely you would find it if you looked in the right place."

The look I got was full of pity, but Jimmie changed the subject. "This is Forfar we are coming to," he said, "and this end of it is called Sheriff Gardens."

"James," I said "you are a very encyclopedia but you are not quite correct. It is called Sheriff Park Gardens, but how do you know so much about it?"

"Because I went with a woman who lived there for years," he answered.

I pulled into the verge, and stopped. "This has put a different complexion on things altogether," I said, "I picked you up in good faith as a Christian would — you said you were not married, now you tell me that you went with this woman for years and I have little doubt that you used her to the full — I have a good mind to take you back to where I got you only I'm running short of petrol — have you anything to say before I put you out right here?"

"What you say is true," he said and then, "But I've left her everything I have in my will. She married another chap. I suppose I took her too much for granted."

"Jimmie," said I, "my faith in you is restored. I am to stop at the Police Station, but do not be afraid, all will be well."

The young constable at the desk asked what he could do for me. I explained how my friend had been left at Perth on the pensioners' bus outing and how his annual holiday in Orkney depended on his being ready next morning in Aberdeen.

"How about getting one of our patrol cars to take him to the boundary with Grampian, and get them to contact the Grampian Police to take him home," I said — the boys meet anyway to exchange notes.

"There should not be any bother about that, Mr Findlay," said the excellent young man. "That's part of our job, to help people."

I regarded him with some awe. "I like everything about you," I said, "but how did you know my name?"

"That's another part of our job," he said, "knowing things" and addressed himself to Jimmie. "Would you like a cup of tea while we wait for the car?" he asked. "We'll manage fine now, Mr Findlay, if you want away home."

A BIRD IN THE BUSH

It was the second Friday in September either 1934 or 1935 and we had had the usual satisfactory trade for our shearlings at Kelso, but what made it unusual was that my father had told me that the Barrs of Upper Dalhousie had invited me to spend the weekend with them to see their farm and to take me to the zoo on Saturday night, and that he was willing to let me go. I wondered what had come over the old boy — there were no holidays for shepherds or ploughmen in those days. I had worked seven days a week since 1931 when I left the Morgan Academy at the age of thirteen, and so I agreed forthwith to go to the Barrs in case he changed his mind. The Barr family had been neighbours of ours at Newtyle and we had developed a close friendship which endures to this day. Robert, who was in the same class as me at school, but always a place or two further up, shared in the boyhood ongoings of the time. W.H., as his father was known, had taken the tenancy of this huge outfit in Midlothian — fourteen pairs was rumoured though nobody at home could believe it, even Auchtertyre had only six pair and an orrabeast, and the house it was said was as big as the Davidson Steading. Little wonder that I was anxious to verify all this, so with a feeling similar to that which Columbus must have had, I went home with the Barrs, to be welcomed like another member of the family.

Jessie and her mother had, like all other farming women, prepared the food for the returning warriors, and after a wash and a meal we spent the evening cracking in front of the fire, mostly about Newtyle, for my hosts were eager to hear about all their old acquaintances. Was the new chap in Davidson doing the right things? Had the glen calves summered well? Was I still playing tennis, was Hugo Johnston still taking his father's motor bike when he was attending a patient? Dr Johnston was the local Medico and Hugo was his youngest son, the same age as Robert and me. He was practically out of control, which way incidentally he stayed for the rest of his life.

When we had spoken about everything we could think of including who had won the shortbread class at the Horticultural Show, and when my eyelids were in need of props we retired for the night, Robert conducting me upstairs round bends and along corridors to my room, and I knew I had at least confirmed one of the things I had heard — this was one hell of a size of a house.

If nobody ever wrote: "Oh sleep, it is a blessed thing," I am pleased to be the one who has done it, and when you are seventeen or so and tired it happens really quickly. I have often watched my own children asleep all relaxed and at peace, all the engines shut off and the recharging process in operation, getting ready for the next release of energy.

Next morning when Robert had shouted for me and I reported downstairs, the women had the breakfast waiting. No cornflakes in these days, but steaming porridge and cream for starters, followed by ham and egg — nobody had ever heard of bacon, — at least not the country folk who worked the three pig system, one in the cleeks, one in the lum and one in the crae. The best cured ham I ever tasted is found at Cormuir in Prosen where George and Mary McIntosh presided over many a meal which could only be described as a banquet and you had to finish clipping before eating because you could not bend afterwards. Their son Stewart and his wife Frances have inherited the art which is one reason why their tea shop is so popular. Be that as it may, after breakfast — by the way W.J. always asked blessing before eating — I was taken round the farm. Ye Gods, it was all true, the stable was so long that it had three hayhouses, and had electricity in it. We had put in electricity at Hatton in 1933 and I thought we were years ahead of anybody else, but Dalhousie had their own generator — of which more anon. The long row of cotter houses with its curious kinks in the roof line was the first time I had ever seen the effects of subsidence from mine working, and the thought that hundreds or thousands of feet below me men were working at that very moment, digging away with a lamp fixed on to their head, made me reflect on the benefits of herding the Hatton of Newtyle, and what an influence what and where you were born had on your life. There is much to be looked at on 1,000 acres. We looked at the horses coming home from the harvest at dinner time, we looked at the young flock of Border Leicesters founded at Davidson from ours, and which was later to produce the mighty Barrticular, we looked at the garden which even had greenhouses and which had in more prosperous times even had a tennis court.

The day wore on until it was time to get ready for the afternoon and evening entertainment — a visit to the zoo, tea in a restaurant and the movies in the evening. It was to be a foursome. Robert was already going steady, as they say, with a girl named Margaret Hunter, whose father farmed not far away, and who Robert went to collect and then returned for Jessie and me. Jessie is about a year different from me in age, was devoted to her parents, expert in every aspect of house work, cooking, embroidery — but did not participate in activities such as dancing a waltz or any other that could be termed loose or permissive in any way.

Of course, the zoo was interesting, the high tea in Crawfords tasty, and the singing of Jeanette MacDonald and Nelson Eddy or Clark Gable and Myrna Loy, or whoever, was beautiful. It was at this time that ''Smilin' Through'' was packing them in, and the four of us naturally rejoiced with a full heart at the inevitable victory of good over evil, and the triumph of true love over impossible odds.

When we set off for home it was late — the breath of autumn was on the wind and there were no heaters in cars those days. To ensure the comfort of the passengers however, most cars had rugs of ample proportions on the back seat, which could be used if occasion demanded like a blanket, and spread over the lap and legs of the travellers. The front of the car was not so bad because you got the heat off the engine — at least there never seemed to be rugs in the front.

Robert was not putting off, and I was not long in noticing that when rounding a right hand bend I was having to resist being thrown against Jessie, and that she was not pushing me away as hard as I expected, so my resistance got lower and lower, and the pair of us snuggled together real friendly like. Alas, our contentment was interrupted by Robert saying that we were now at the end of the drive, and if we would get out he would run Margaret home, which process would take about three quarters of an hour. He did not want us to go into the house because if we switched on a light the generator engine would start up and waken up the old folk who were the better of uninterrupted rest, so if we took the rug to keep warm he would pick us up when he came back, and we could all go in together.

So there were the two of us standing at the garden gate, and I was holding the rug watching the tail light getting smaller, with no chance of its returning for forty-four and a half minutes. I spread the rug on the ground in the shelter of a huge shrub, and we sat down to wait. It is not easy when you are eighteen, well fed and rested, to sit quiet in the dark beside a lovely girl, feeling the warmth of her and smelling the perfume that makes you dizzy. I suppose one should exercise self discipline and pray for help to overcome. I have tried both without much success, although I have to admit I have noticed a marked improvement recently.

Both of us I fear were fighting a losing battle, but fate in the shape of Robert's return, happily prevented us from breaking one or other of the commandments which used to attract the penalty of death by stoning. Composing ourselves as best we could we rejoined the chauffeur, but not before I had told my girl that I was sure to suffer a severe headache about a quarter of an hour after going to bed, and if she could bring along an aspirin or two it would help me to get to sleep. She promised right away and I kissed her in appreciation of her concern for my comfort.

Before going upstairs we had a cup of cocoa or Horlicks or something, with the bump, bump of the generator motor grinding away in the washing house, and I thought their father and mother must be sound sleepers if they could sleep through that. However either they did sleep or they offered no comment on the behaviour of their children burning electricity at two in the morning. After ages, and with my hand on my temple and a look in Jessie's direction I was conducted by Robert to my room and said goodnight. The warmth of the room and the adequacy of the blankets persuaded me to divest myself of my clothing and I switched off the light and got into bed to await events. In due course the engine went silent, an indication that the last lamp was out, and the countdown began. There I was lying in a condition usually associated with a butcher's dog, listening as I had seldom listened before for sound of the door being opened. At last I was sure I heard the faintest sound, and I knew that it was being shut, for I had made sure that the catch was not engaged.

"Over here, dear," I whispered and threw down the bed clothes. There was a silence. "Jessie," I said again in a whisper. "You will need to bring them here; my head is about bursting." Still nothing. "You wee rascal," I said, "I'm coming to get you," and I got out of bed. Feeling my way along the wall, I navigated myself round the room, past dressing tables, wardrobes and chairs, but never a hand could I lay on my lovely temptress. Again I whispered, "If this is some kind of a game, I would like to know the rules; for any sake get into bed before we are both frozen." I might as well have spoken to the wind. "Jessie," I said, "This is going too far, I am standing with my hand on the switch and if you don't come to me before ten I will put on the light."

Even as I spoke, I knew I had blown it if things went wrong, but I was too excited to care. At the drop of the switch the clatter of the motor shattered the stillness, and the room was flooded with light. There I was, standing stark naked beside the closed door, absolutely alone in the room. Still unbelieving, I went over and opened the door of the wardrobe just in case. Convinced at last, I crossed the room again to put out the light, and it was then that I saw the two little white tablets lying on the floor just inside the door. I have often wondered since where things started to go right or wrong, whichever way you look at it. Even the title of this story could be one of a few. The angler would call it "The one that got away", the philosopher; : "So near and yet so far", the novelist: "Holiday gone Haywire", but I can at least say with complete conviction that "A Bird in the Bush" is worth more than one in a bedroom where the chances of getting in beside her parents by mistake are 50:50.

... A SAUSAGE BY ITS SKIN

There is an unwritten law that you only get so long at the top. It is unwritten because no-one can explain this phenonemon, but the fact remains that no matter how hard you try you will come clatter sometime if you stay on long enough. Naturally, I do not propose to give examples, as relatives of nearly every famous herd or flock of the past might dispute this statement on behalf of their own ancestor while agreeing with all the other examples.

I had a spell when I suppose I could be classified as one of the élite in both Blackfaces and Border Leicesters, and certainly when I handed over the Border Leicester flock to Marcus it was out on its own, invariably topping whichever sale it was represented at, but my time with the Blackfaces had run out, and I was struggling a bit. Whether it is because young men come up with the enthusiasm and ambition to establish their niche and the public respond to youth, or whether a flock reflects its owner's vitality, I just do not know, but once you start slipping you cannot do anything about it. You can buy the four most expensive tups of the year; you can even buy in ewes from a top flock and it will not make any difference — the only thing to do is to hand over to your next of kin and get the joy of seeing them come surging back. The Border Leicester breed lends itself to intelligent sire selection far more than the Blackface, for several reasons. One is that there is only one universally recognised type. The Blackfaces have at least three, which have been interbred, resulting in far too many of them being scattered breeders with their lambs identifying with their diverse ancestry. The Leicesters, however, whose pedigrees one can trace for a hundred years, can be relied on to sire lambs which bear a true resemblance to their sire, so that the gifted stockbreeder can select strains to strengthen particular characteristics within a pretty well predestined whole. There is alleged to be something about an outstanding breeder that the master stockman recognises and that is what sets him apart from his less favoured rivals, but I dispute this theory. I think that once a beast has demonstrated his ability everybody then credits his appearance and behaviour as belonging to an ace, but it is my belief that many potential top notchers never get a chance.

It is easy to provide proof that physical excellence has little to do with genetic ability, and to provide such proof I instance the Hazelside tup Standfast, commonly regarded as probably the greatest specimen of our time. He went round the shows unbeaten in his class, and unbeaten as a male. First at the Highland as a lamb — then as a shearling — and as an aged ram. Champion at Biggar, first at Lanark. As the time for him coming into the sale ring approached the atmosphere was electric. He made £2,200, after various syndicates had made pre-sale bargains about who would bid and who would not, who would get five ewes to him, and who would get him when he was three shear and so on. He really was so good that people did not have the heart to bid for him, although £2,200 was indeed a lot of money in the early sixties. I was one who chickened that day and I do not know why; he was the only tup of either breed that I wanted and did not buy. He went to Robert Hamilton of Cobbinshaw, and we all waited to see his lambs — but alas, they were no better than those of anybody else, nor did those of the next year show any improvement. Nevertheless hardly a day passed but what I thought about him, and longed to own him. Then one day Dougal and I were working among the shearlings in the pens at Hatton. It was a fine day in late July, really warm, and as usual we were talking sheep. After a lengthy silence I remarked, "I wonder if Robert Hamilton would sell Standfast?"

Dougal looked across. "I would not have believed it," he said "I was wondering exactly the same thing."

"That's it then," I said, "I'll go down and buy him."

About three hours later, I landed at Cobbinshaw where I found Robert turning hay. I told him what I was about and asked him to put a price on him.

"If you buy him, you will be sorry," Robert said, "He really is a bad breeder."

"Robert," says I, "Let me worry about that. I am sure he will suit our ewes and I really am keen to have him."

"Very well then, £250 and remember I warned you."

We gave him our best eighty ewes, and waited to prove that if you were as good as he was you were bound to breed. Alas, Robert had understated the brute. We got black lambs, spotted lambs, pigmented lambs — it was a nightmare — but at least there were some that seemed all right, so we showed him at the Highland to let people see the sort of rams we used. The result was as usual. He got Male Champion, and crowds round him all week, and one of his lambs was second in his class as well. His mongrel ancestry was not finished with us yet though. By the time his sons were shearlings they were disgraceful with long beards and drift locks, more hair than wool, and those of them that got the length of a sale could hardly be given away. I put him to the second Stirling sale where as usual he got first prize and Tom Mitchell of Gateside bought him for £160 in spite of my warning and again as usual, he nearly put Tom out of business. Yet, even today, nearly a quarter of a century later, I can see him yet. He made the championship of any show a foregone conclusion, and when I was beside him he gave me an inferiority complex, the only beast, or body either for that matter, that ever did.

I once got a dressing down from an irate father for persuading his son to join the Army. He said that his son was too delicate for such activity, and that his mother was not well as a result of my actions. When I tried to assure him that Derek was a big strong boy who would do really well, he would have none of it.

"There is one bloody thing I want you to get into your head," he said, "Never judge a sausage by its skin, and if there's a war and he gets killed I'll curse you for the rest of my life."

THERE IS PLENTY OF ROOM AT THE TOP

In choosing this title I am quoting a much used and over-estimated exhortation which parents and other well wishers use to inspire greater effort from their progeny. They blissfully overlook the fact that everybody else is up to the same trick, and the final place in the pecking order is usually established by luck, perhaps because the individual concerned has had very intelligent parents, or because he has inherited a farm from a batchelor uncle who had made a fortune in Assam. The attribute which spurred me to wherever I got was pride, and I got it from my father. Getting second at anything was little short of a tragedy.

Imagine therefore how I felt after selling my first rams at Kelso, and getting almost the lowest average of the sale. The fact that I had been absent for three years, and people forget quickly, and that I had been training soldiers practically every night all year did not matter a damn. I could hardly bear to tell my mother the sale result. I had a good think about things and decided to proclaim to the world straight away who was the best breeder of Border Leicesters, and on the Sunday following my disaster I made my way to Lanark determined to buy what I thought would be the top priced ram. The fizz was on about two — Alan Howie's Eshott Brooks No 1 and Knockdon's No 1. I liked Alan Howie's the better and bought him for a new record price for a ram of £340. The record lasted less than half an hour, when Bob Forrest of Preston gave Sandy Burns £360 for the Knockdon one. I got home to Hatton at one o'clock in the morning but my mother heard me coming upstairs.

"Did you buy anything?" she asked from her bed. I knew I would have to go gently.

"Yes, Mum. I got one from Alan Howie."

"Are you pleased with him?" she asked.

"Oh yes, I think he is just what we need," I answered.

"What did he cost?"

It had to come. "Well, Mum, he was dear, £340."

There was a long silence then, and I can hear her yet: "My God!" It was not an oath or blasphemy — I never heard my mother even say damn — it was an appeal to him who stills the storm to guide her only son and to prosper his aims and ambitions. Nor was her supplication in vain. I named the ram Carefree, and his first crop of sons in Kelso returned one of the highest averages of the sale, although as mentioned elsewhere Bob Adam got the highest price off him — the new record of £550. That one beast — my declaration of intent — was the single most important event that opened the doors for me to be accepted by the greatest stocksmen of our generation, men like Ben Wilson, John Cassidy, Jim Brown, Jim McCutcheon, Robert Paterson, David and Andrew Provan, Willie Mitchell, Niven Paterson, Bob Adam, Alan Grant, John McGillivray, J.E. Kerr, Jim Durno, Watt Taylor, Sandy Stewart, Robbie Weir, Jacob Horner, Robbie Mulligan and on and on. All these and more like them had managed to find room at the top, and knowing them is a rewarding experience. All of them had one common factor which got them where they are or were, and that common factor is luck.

I would like to relate what was probably my first acquaintance with Lady Luck. One forenoon in August 1919 the Marcus Kelso shearlings were being washed. The wash box was a wooden one shaped like a huge bath and it was set beside the lade, some forty yards upstream from the water wheel that drove the threshing mill, so readers will understand the force of the rushing water. When the rams were properly scrubbed the soap was rinsed out by pouring bucketfuls of water over them from the lade. Elsewhere I refer to the water in the lade when I quote Hamewith's *The Packman.* My mother gave me the milk tanker to help in this job, which was done by my father and the shepherd who was at this time the then young Sandy Burns, later of Knockdon, who ended his distinguished herding career at Seaton of Usan with David Alston. It shows the tolerance of my father that he put up with a three year old for I must have been more of a hinder than a help. To fill my tanker from the lade I had to lie down and stretch out my arm to reach the water which I would then pour over the tup in the bath. This time I overbalanced and fell head first into the lade, and was carried off downstream just like a bit of stick. The next thing I remember was Sandy Burns pulling me out, only about three yards from the mill wheel. Another ten seconds and I would have had it, for there was no way down to the bottom, some fourteen feet deep and drained by an underground conduit. I am sure that Sandy prevented a double fatality that day because my father would have jumped into the wheel to try to save me. His shouting brought my mother running out to see what was wrong and she led me away to the house to dry me. I remember as if it was yesterday the pools of water on the kitchen floor when I was being stripped. All through my life I have held Sandy Burns in special regard for saving me that day and I think that when things were going my way in the sheep world that Sandy shared the satisfaction that success brings.

Once at a post-sale celebration when some were congratulating me about Prince of Angus or Bow Tie, or Barrticular or Angus Supreme, Sandy got things into proper prospective. "You can count me in on this too, lads, for if it wasn't for me Jim wouldna be here."

I am sure that if I conclude this little incident with a plea to all parents to teach their children to swim, someone may sometime bless reading this page. This was one bad omission in my childhood days and it was brought home to me when I sailed to France in a troop ship with a fair chance of being torpedoed by one of Admiral Donitz's submarines. I resolved if we landed safely the first thing I would do would be to correct this deficiency and I learned to swim in the French miners' pithead baths.

I do not suppose it would have made any difference if we had been sunk in mid-Channel, but the sea has seemed a whole lot friendlier ever since.

The big event in our life when Sandy Burns was shepherd came in 1920 when dad sold his No 1 Marcus Eclipse for £1,100, an all British tup record, and one that lasted for nearly thirty years. I think that Willie Mitchell, of Bank House, Kelso put £100 on to it before I got it back with King of Angus in 1950, and gave the rest a target to aim at. Then in my last year in 1976 I got £6,000 for Angus Golden Promise. I still have the telegram which was sent from Kelso to acquaint us at home of the great tidings, for in 1920 £1,100 would have bought a street of houses or a small farm. The foreman Adam Reid's reaction to the news has remained a kind of family saying every time we have had a good price for a tup or a pen of stirks — "Maybe I'll get a new set of plough chains now, I'm ashamed to take anybody into the stable."

In those days there were plenty of people on the land, one man to fifty acres, a pair of horses to seventy, and of an evening in summer you could have twenty coming in about to putt the shot and throw the hammer in the stackyard, sometimes to play quoits — a thing I have not seen for over fifty years. Some played the fiddle, some the melodian, others the mouthorgan, even the trump had its exponents. The means of transport was bicycle with the musical instrument carried in its case slung over the shoulder, and of course the steading was critically examined for tidiness and maintenance. Hence Adam's reception of the news about Eclipse. From what I was told, Eclipse was the outstanding exhibit in 1920 so my father must have known the same thrill as I was lucky enough to experience about ten times when one of mine was pulling in the big boys at the principal sale of the year. Of course I had two breeds, so I had double the chances. I do not think it is the prospect of getting a big price that starts up the butterflies, it is the dread of something going wrong at the last second, and as early as 1945 I was dreaming of such disaster.

Carefree's first crop was eagerly anticipated turning up at the sales, and I thought they were good. No 1 was a wild rascal, and in the summer had split open his head fighting and I had him shut in a shed to bathe him and to keep the flies off him. To add to the atmosphere when people came to see him, I had a bowl of roses on the windowsill and I used to catch him by extending a rose at full arm's length then grabbing him while he was smelling it. People used to ask if I had him trained at anything else, and at Kelso I decided to let the world see what could be done. After the auctioneer had introduced him, I requested to be allowed to demonstrate his versatility. First I caught him with the rose, then let him go and held up my hand for silence for his pièce de résistance. "Lie down and die," I commanded, and he stretched himself out prostrate in the middle of the ring. The applause was tumultuous and photographers crawled round the motionless beast. At last the auctioneer asked the ring to be cleared and indicated that the time had come to sell.

"That'll do," I ordered, "Get up now," but there was no response. I approached him and pushed him with my foot, but horror of horrors there was still no result. Frantic with fear I pulled him about the ring, but the tell tale froth at his nostril demonstrated that he had obeyed me all too well. I am unaware if anyone has died as a result of a heart attack actually occurring in a dream; when one is thirty-odd the heart can take a fair load, but now at 66 I am quite certain that if I have another dream like that, it will be the finish of me. I wonder if the obituary will start "Peacefully in his sleep," for I have yet to see one start "Suddenly as the result of a dream."

Elsewhere I have told readers of the mystery of why if you let one of your pals get a female or two to your stud sire, he will get the best son. Now another vivid example comes readily to mind. I had bred a son of Carefree out of an outstanding ewe called Queen of Angus, and decided he was too good to sell. I took in forty ewes to him from eight of the best bred flocks, and retained the right to buy any tup lamb for £100 — a big price in these days. The one I chose was bred at Newhouse, and I named him Beacon of Angus. His mother was a really good ewe, BL 66 FU 5, by a ram bred by my uncle Harry, and named Dalama. Harry had been in Africa making his pile and Dalama was Zulu for gold. With ancestors like his Beacon could not be other than a great breeder and his first crop included the new record breaker King of Angus. No 2 that day was sold to Robert Stewart of Millerhill at £120 and my old friend Robert Barr got two ewes to him. Sure enough, next year at Lanark Robert Barr turned up with the one everybody wanted. To add to the drama he was carrying his off fore foot and with everybody being at him was having a rough time. Robert thought that I could possibly locate the sore bit and possibly give him relief. As I suspected it was a bealing foot and I managed to lance it. Before I let him up I said to Robert:

"Bob, he is running a hell of a temperature, I think you should insure him for a year to the buyer."

I knew that it was going to be me.

After I bought him for £1,000, the new ram lamb record, I reminded Robert of his promise. "What will it cost?" he asked, £90 I answered, 9% of the purchase price. Bob's answer was not original, but it was apt. "You are hardly for decent folk to live with — this takes the gilt off the gingerbread — but I promised and I will perform."

Big Business, Champion FHAS 1963 Sold for £2,300

I think that the tup that created almost as much interest as Standfast in the Blackface world was Big Business. Rumours had been circulating all summer that Woolfords had a good one and a number of us visited the Hamiltons to see for ourselves. Jim Brown of Kirklandbank was my idol as a Blackface stocksman in these days, and incidentally he stayed that way all his life but that day we did not agree on the best one. I thought a blackheaded one was what was needed but Jim agreed with those who were on the raw looking brocket face shearling that was bringing a constant stream of visitors. I decided not to follow the crowd and to buy my own favourite —

they were both by the same sire and I thought I would be left with more change anyway. Alas, when I got to Lanark the situation had changed. There was no argument now. The black one had gone back, his hair had gone, his coat was broken — I hardly recognised him, while his rival stood out head and shoulders as the star of the sale. He cost me £2,200 while Willie Lindsay of Robiesland paid £180 for my original choice. Jean Hamilton wanted me to call mine BignBraw, but I had already christened him Big Business. He was the popular choice as the best ram to date. He went unbeaten throughout his show career, he was my first Highland champion and is the society's choice for the frontpiece of its official handbook to this day. I need hardly add that the money spinner was Willie Lindsay's. He sold tups over £1,000 off his on several occasions, while Big Business although a great breeder of females never bred one £1,000 offspring. If I had let somebody get five ewes to him he would have, but I was wise to this trick of fate and operated the closed shop idea. He really was a good stock beast, his daughters milked like Ayrshire cows, they had great frames and constitution. I used him and his sons on all the farms I had. He spent his last two years at Doonies in Glenisla and was finally killed at nine shear by a garron mare called Blossom, who broke his back while he was eating out of a trough and she ran in on him with the fore feet.

I spoke to a farmers' gathering one winter's night in Tobermory, the capital of Islay, and I was advising them to be good to their ewes, to feed them in storms, to dip them and dose them so their life could be happy. I ended with a message in rhyme from the beasts themselves:

Just one more boon we humbly crave
If you want to get the best that is in us
There's one thing sure our lambs should be:
Related to Big Business.

THE SECOND OLDEST PROFESSION

Livestock management is a discipline which has been with us for a bit longer than most of us imagine. When at school we hear about Mendel and his beans and the revolutionary theories of Charles Darwin. I assumed that these fellows were pioneers in their trade, so it came as a bit of a shock to read that some 3,000 years BC, Tutankamun, the boy Pharoah, sent one of his governers to restore some order in Nubia which had been giving the "Lord of the two countries" a bit of bother with some nonsense about independence from Egypt. The new Viceroy set about his work enthusiastically, personally supervising arts ranging from gold mining and cabinet making to selective animal breeding. In the 1940's there was much argument about this new thing called artificial insemination; we now know that the Arabs used this method of selective breeding as standard practice in the days of the Crusaders. For all I know this was one of the improved techniques that Huy introduced to the Nubians all these fifty centuries ago.

Even as animals are selectively bred, so by association with them are their owners. Stockmen the world over are a breed of their own, and mix with their kind. Their children grow up together, mate and reproduce and so continue the line of humans with an inborn skill in animal management, made dominant by generations of ancestors all with whatever genes hand down this particular ability. In one of my idler moments I traced back my paternal ancestry in the records branch at Edinburgh. I found seven generations before closing time. They were all farmers in the glens of Angus, marrying amongst others game-keepers' daughters who learned Latin and Greek which had been taught in byres and stables by some distinguished native of advanced years who had returned to his homeland after a career in the great centres of learning of the world. In 1835 there were over 200 children of school age in Glenesk; you can see the records in Retreat Museum; today there are less than fifty, and the country is the poorer for it.

What I want to record in this chapter is some of the events and animals I have encountered in my 63 years up till now. The first animal I can remember was a black cow named Jan, and she stood on the left side of a stall in the byre at Marcus Mill about the year 1919. I went with my mother to the milking in the evenings and when mother was milking Bell, who was the other occupant of the stall, I tried to milk Jan. I had a small tanker to catch my milk in and with my one free hand I generally had enough to feed the cats by the time mother had finished Bell and was ready for Jan. They must, I now realise, have been two very well mannered cows to allow a three year old to dotter about beside them the way they did, and I am grateful that my first association with cattle was such a happy one.

My favourite hen as a child, was a deep red coloured matron of uncertain pedigree. My mother allowed her favourite hens to set themselves, and she kept the pullets from these selected dams. Wally — named because she always nested beside the well in the garden from whence we drew our water — was the queen of the farmyard, clean legged, bright eyed. She laid on after the others were dry, and had the knack of often being in the right place at the right time to get a bite of any piece I had got. She loved raspberry jam, so we had that much in common. She was a very devoted mother to her chicks when they were little and attacked anything or anybody who got too near them. She actually killed a full grown rat which was foolish enough to invade her territory at the time her chicks were hatching. She lived a long life; we took her with us when we flitted to Hatton in 1927. I cannot remember her eventual demise, but by this time I was ten, and young men of that age cannot be seen to be interested in hens. She remains forever in my memory as an example of three virtues — courage, endurance and energy.

The first sheep I can remember, and the memory is crystal clear, was the Border Leicester ewe BL409Z24. It would be either 1925 or 1926 that I got to know her, for at lambing time she was kept in the cow park beside the house — she had so much milk that we milked her whenever a hungry lamb needed help. Mother could get a bottleful from her every day, and for years she was the provider of the substance we know now as colostrum. We did not know the name of it in those days, but we knew that hungry lambs that got her milk lived and ones that did not died. She, like Wally, made the trip to Hatton in 1927, and she was the mother of Hatton Flockmark in 1928. He was, I think the top priced ram in Kelso in 1929, and was sold for £205 to Messrs. Wallace of Auchenbrain, Machline. If he passed on to his daughters what his mother had to him, whoever herded the Auchenbrain flock was bound to bless him. I did not bless him though, for when he came home from the Highland Show at Alloa where he was second in his class, one of his knees swelled up and the vet ordered a half hour daily of a cold water hose run on to it. I got this job and nightly after school I had to stand and let the water run down his leg for what seemed an eternity, for I could hear and sometimes see the rest of the children playing football in the close or bools or cricket with a home made bat and a rubber ball. It was all worth it though, for he was sold sound, and £205 would just about pay six months rent of the 707 acres that was Hatton at that time.

The first Blackface that I remember was born in 1926, and was the first sheep I owned. The tup lambs from Braco, our other farm in Lethnot, came down to Marcus for the wintering but were put to Craigend of Careston up till the new year, and I had to look them every night on my way home from school. As this required a journey of about a mile in the wrong direction from my home I got my mother's bicycle to speed things up. I could not, of course, reach the seat but I was the envy of the rest of the children as I pedalled along like the clappers in a standing position. For my pains my father gave me my pick on the condition that I knew him again after next year's summering. As I was desperate to get a boy's bicycle that I could reach I could not afford an error so I took the only one pure black in the face and fore legs. Even in those days people were kind. He made £22 in Perth in 1927 and I bought my 22''frame bicycle from John Hill, of West High Street, Forfar for six pounds. Little wonder I grew fond of Blackfaces.

By this time too I had my own dog, a bitch out of Stanley Dallas' Fan by my father's Ned. I have told you about the row about the mating, when Stanley alleged that I had let him into the henhouse where she was being kept in isolation but the dog could lift the bole with his nose. I think he must have learned the trick by watching the bothy lads going through the maids' window. Anyway, time healed everything and I got one of the pups and called her Pearl. In the long summer evenings of 1926 the two of us used to hunt the banks of the Noran for water hens and the eggs — I took all the eggs that were not gogged and had them fried. They seemed far better tasted than the produce of Wally and Co, but I now know that this illusion was caused by the feeling of being a successful hunter. Pearl taught me many of the things I have referred to in my bit about dogs; she inherited her father's vice of raking, in fact he taught her the finer parts of the art, such as knowing when to sneak away without being noticed, going conveniently deaf when on the rake, and finally coming home through the night so she could be lying innocently at the back door when her master came out in the morning. She also mastered the art of walking under water and could follow any water hen which attempted escape by this method. She was really hard mouthed and anything she killed was ruined for the pot; she was particularly savage on rats, cats and weasels, and far too sore on sheep that contradicted her. Even after my father cut her teeth level she could still dispose of her victims with an efficiency that I have never since seen equalled.

There are some things that animals do, especially dogs, which are difficult to understand let along explain. My present dog, Fred, follows submerged water rats successfully apparently by scent, but this should be impossible.

As the years go by I find myself becoming more and more convinced of the veracity of some of the hitherto unbelievable exploits of James Hogg's Hector and Sirrah related in the glorious Tales of an Ettrick Shepherd. Old Andrew Lindsay of Tipperty, a friend of my father's insisted that his half-husky "Stalin" counted the tups every morning to save going round the field if they were all at the troughs.

How I wish that I had had a tape recorder during Andrew's visits to us. My father and he were forever arguing on matters pastoral — of dogs and tods and heather besoms, home made scythe sneds and ever and ever about sheep. In appearance Andrew, heavily bearded long before it became fashionable, always conjured up in my mind a picture of one of the disciples at least, and somewhat timidly I even ventured to think he was very much what Jesus must have been like. He had served throughout the Boer War and told me about how the rascals tried to get you tangled up in barbed wire and then raked it with machine guns firing fixed line. He said he had escaped once by undoing his belt and leaving his kilt firmly stuck in the wire. He had complete dominance over animals. He bred bulls, and they all knew him all their lives — the same with tups — they would stand in a field while he clipped them, a process which would take about an hour, but Andrew was never in a hurry. The hillmen of his day belonged to an age now gone. Long nights at the cards, the bottle on the table and often they got home about the time that we were getting up. That was one advantage of the pony and trap over the car, a good shelt would always come home itself and the wife had only to help you from the stable.

Andrew's mother died at the age of 99 years, 11 months and 2 weeks, and she had been keeping house right up to the end. Andrew missed her a lot and retired to a lonely house in a field at Auchenblae, where one morning the postman found him dead. He had been dead for some time and the post-mortem diagnosed malnutrition. There was no food in the house. We think he had hurt himself somehow and been unable to get help or provision. His passing was a sharp reminder to me of our responsibility for the aged.

After we came to Hatton in 1927 I chummed up with the gamekeeper's two sons Arthur and Jim Coates, and the three of us would catch up to twenty rabbits any night after school on Hatton Hill. Nearly every whin bush had a flap in it and Pearl hunted with one foot up as expertly as any setter or spaniel. All we had to do was to poke the whin with our sticks, and she disposed of the occupant as it emerged. At her best she never missed. I think it is worth recording an incident some three years later when I was herding for my father. I was coming home one day after looking the hill, and Pearl set at a small whin no bigger than a bothy pot. As was my wont I jumped on top of it to either kill or dislodge the rabbit. Imagine my horror when I found I had fatally injured a partridge sitting on a clutch of eggs. I shoved the dead bird into a rabbit burrow and thanked God that nobody had witnessed so foul a deed. When I got down to the farm my father was cracking to Jim Coates senior, who had been down at the estate office, so I knew I had been unobserved.

Some days later the other herd, Jock Robertson, told me that Coates had asked him if I had told him anything about killing a partridge in a whin not far from the water tank. I had told nobody, so Jock was unable to help him.

"What I think has happened," the keeper said, "was that that damned bitch of his had set at the whin and Jim had belted it with his stick thinking it was a rabbit. Anyway, there is no sign of the hen and most of the eggs are broken.''

Jim Coates was a good man. He never challenged me about it and I am glad he didn't because I might have denied it and the guilt would be with me still.

Pearl spent her declining years with the Messrs. Wyllie at Kilnaniel, much loved and cared for. I have her kind to this day through John Skeldon's Georgie, Jim Wilson's Craig, Home Riggs Ben, my Roy and Alan Perrie's Jean. If there is a better kind I do not know of them.

If I return to Hatton Flockmark for a moment, it is to relate the great fear that my father had in August 1929, that he was to lose the wool on his scrotum or cod as we usually call it, and the few locks that adhered up to saletime were as pearls of great price. Thirty years later I was doing my best to breed a kind with no wool there as we had by now discovered that semen was better stored in a cool place and the first thing anybody did was to remove any such wool in the interest of fertility. Flockmark was a son of the tough old sire Ardo Flockmark, whose strength was the substance of my father's taunt any time I let a beast rise in the dipper, even at my best: "I doubt he's an Ardo Flockmark."

I would need to spend some time hereabout on my acquaintance with horses because at the age of thirteen my greatest ambition was to drive a pair, and my father (wisely I think) let me do so for one year aged fourteen.

I left Morgan Academy at the summer holidays of 1930 with a very average academic achievement, determined to have the cleanest harness and best groomed pair in the parish. It was not easy, for the foreman David Guild had the same idea, and his father did not come out at 10 o'clock at night and order him home to bed and if he was not in the stable every night it was because he had taken a bit of harness home with him. His pair, Punch and Clyde, were far abler than mine, Rose and Tam, and Dave himself never let up. After a day at the dung I could hardly stay awake with fatigue, but I knew that he would never be any stronger and I would. I do not think I know as much about horses as plenty of other people — one heard whispers about the horseman's grip and the horseman's word and being made a horseman at some midnight ritual where after much horseplay you were endowed with horse sense, but the parental pressure was always being applied and my destiny was with sheep and cattle, so I bowed to the inevitable and took up herding.

By this time cross Highland cows were established on Hatton Hill so I had to learn the cattle job as well. The reintroduction of cows on hills was a new concept in mixed farming in 1930 and those of us involved learned the hard way. We had a stock, I suppose, of about thirty out of which about twenty-five would attack you for about three weeks after calving, and as they left their calves hidden in bracken or rushes you had to be very careful where you went. Fortunately Hatton Hill was not drained at that time and so long as you could beat them to a marsh you could get the better of them. Many's the dirty brute I have choked unconscious after I got her bogged. It was only after one of them savaged my father in 1939 that I resolved never again to keep a cow liable to attack humans. Perhaps most of you people who work with cattle already know this — you get about twenty seconds notice when a cattle beast is to attack, if you are close to it. Its eyes will gradually bulge in its sockets, and when you see this happening either knock it down or run for cover. I discovered this useful information while towing a cross Highlander behind a Landrover, and every time her eyes bulged she tried to get at me in the back. Cattle seem to beselective as to who they are to attack, like bees choosing who to sting, but the real outlaws will have a go at anybody, and the only answer is a shot. Just as in humans, every animal species has its various different natured members; the ill-tempered ones, the docile ones, the generous ones, the timid ones, the clever ones, the dull ones, the long sighted ones, the gluttons and the choosy ones, the caring mothers and the careless ones. If humans have them so do beasts.

One example of an animal whose trust in me was explicit was when I was taking my great Lincoln bull to sell at Perth. I led him into the Landrover trailer; his great weight was too much for the floor and both his forefeet went through. The great chap did not panic, but allowed me to help him out and I tied him to a post while I got a door to lay over the weak floorboards. He did not question my decision and entered the trailer with complete confidence and trust. I felt a real heel selling so noble an animal. I did so because my calf buyer said he wanted calves by an AA bull. Sure as fate, next year he said that he had been wrong about the Lincolns — what great cattle they had turned.

I would not care to say whether he or the cross Highland cow we milked for a decade or so was my favourite cattle beast. I was on the hill that day and saw her as a heifer with a calf's head and one leg sticking out of her. I always carried a rope and tied her to a big stone so that I could help her to calve. It was not very difficult, but alas the calf was not breathing. I was massaging away at it like you always do for about five minutes after you know very well it is dead and miracles do not happen very often but I loosed off the cow when I was beat. She started to clean the calf so energetically that I thought I detected a movement and greatly daring I knelt down beside it to pump its legs once more. Instead of objecting, the great cow included me in her maternal actions. She licked my hands and arms, my shirt, anything that had the smell of the calf, and I promised her there and then she would be my house cow as long as she lived, and that I would keep all her heifer calves in the herd. I tell you, she never lifted a foot all the years I milked her and one of her daughters, Silver, regularly had my top stot calf. Silver was bulled as a calf and never grew very big — year after year her calf was bigger than herself when we speaned him at 10 months. Although Highland's daughters were all quite well mannered none of them could compare with their mother in their affection for me and my family, and on reflection I give the cow the award of the cattle beast I have loved the most.

The sheep that earns that distinction is with me now. She is a three crop Blackface ewe called Waterlily owing to her habit as a lamb of wading into the Quharity burn, to devour the leaves of the water lilies which grow in abundance in the stills of the burn. Where she got this habit from I do not know. Neither her brother nor her mother participated and although I warned her time and again of what happened to ewe lambs that waded in hill burns, she persisted and I used to take visitors to see her practically under water chewing away happily. She does it yet, and I have to keep her away from the burn till her lambs are big enough to get out, but as yet I have never seen any of her lambs in the water. I learned something from her just two days ago: sheep recognise each other by sight as well as scent. This year she had a tup lamb and a wether lamb and the wether from quite small always crawled fences to get roadside grass (his waterlilies). I speaned about ten days ago and the roar has been off both ewe and lamb for over a week. On the morning in question the bold boy was back at his tricks on the road, and I sent Fred to correct him for his misbehaviour. Fred usually gives an offender a coup or two, and the lamb knew what was coming and he went down the road like the clappers, clearing a nine foot grid and rejoining the speaned ewes, which I had gathered previously to see if they were all right. I was leaning on the gate waiting to see what would happen when the two got near each other. Waterlily as usual was standing at the gate about four yards from me; she is always nearest although she will not let me actually touch her. Her son gradually wore through the flock until he got to the front, when from about ten yards he saw his mother. He came straight across although neither spoke nor smelled, and touched her neck with his mouth. She acknowledged his presence, but with a gentle shove told him he was a big boy now and could look after himself. She really is a dear — never more so than when being clipped, is not bad to other folk's lambs in the buchts, even takes a dipping without offence. She was the first ewe that Sally actually lambed — she wants me with her at that time and like the cow I have promised her to keep all her ewe lambs. Whoever gets her tup lamb is going to have a very happy herding life if he retains all his daughters.

Here is just a short note on the greatest delicacy that a sheep can get. It is not waterlilies, nor swede turnips nor heather nor kale nor clover, nor rape nor flaked maize, nor locust beans nor linseed cake nor fish meal nor boiled barley nor beet pulp nor dried milk; it is rose petals. I made this discovery long ago when I scattered some refuse from the house which included some roses alleged to be past

Three Blackface sheep at Aucharroch 1972

their best. The petals vanished at once and the ewes scraped amongst what was left till not one remained. I mentioned this to a young man who is at present halfway up the farming ladder, but he already knew. I asked him how he found out and his answer said it all: "The tups once got into my mother's garden in August and that was the first thing they ate."

Animals are queer, just like many other things and I want to give an example of something that always happens and for which I can give no explanation. If you buy a good stud beast and let your friend get one or two females to him he will have the best offspring, and you will never get even till he buys a good one and offers you a ewe or two to him. In 1943 I bought what was then the record priced ram lamb, Carefree, at £340 to let the world know I meant business. A young up and coming farmer named Robert Adam was starting Border Leicesters at the time and wanted to purchase two gimmers from me, in lamb to Carefree. I knew the danger and put on a condition that I thought could not be met. I said they would be sold in Aberdeen and would have to make £30 each before I would tup them. As no gimmers had ever made more than £20 I thought I was safe enough, but I reckoned without my host. Bob simply got one of his pals to run them up and he got them both at exactly £30 each. I had 60 ewes with the tup and Bob had two. One of his lambs made £550 and the other £240. My dearest one from all my flock was £200.

Time rolled on till 1958 in October at Stirling. The tup that many men desired was in the Brackenhirst pen and there was much to-ing and fro-ing going on with combines being formed and all the usual sparring. Bob came to me and after talking about many other things casually asked if I was on the Brackenhirst sheep. Evasively, I replied that I did not know anybody that was not on him and the best man would likely win.

"Well," said Bob, "I am determined to get him and if you stay off him I will give you five ewes to him."

The memory of 1943 flooded back and I made the deal at once. I sold three sons off him from my five ewes at £1,000, £550 and £380. Bob's dearest one was £500. The wheel had turned full circle.

Although this is not a chapter about Robert Adam I have his authority to give one more example of this phenomenon. Bob sold an AA heifer to Tom Todd of Manorhill, and generously put her in calf to his stock bull. The calf Jewvil Eric of Manorhill was the outstanding bull of his year, made £12,000 to Newhouse and three years later was sold for £18,000. The element of chance has played an important part in the evolution of the nations and the animal species, and an example or two of this factor is justified in any thesis of this kind.

In the world of Border Leicester sheep, amongst other serious faults, brown spots of hair on the head or legs are completely unacceptable to top breeders, and many an outstanding sire has been used only for crossing for having a brown spot somewhere or other. I owned a magnificent shearling once, completely devalued because of a brown spot about the size of half a crown of the back of his near hind leg. In spite of his fault I wanted to exhibit him at the county show, and with his fellow exhibits I took him to the dipper to wash him. When I turned him on his back into the tank he went berserk and threshed the water with his hind legs in an absolute frenzy. I refused to let him up and the battle continued till I knew that if I held him down any longer he was a goner. When he was going up the dipper I noticed blood running down his leg where he had been flailing away against the edge of the stone dipper. Closer examination showed that he was minus his brown spot, skin and all, so nea'.y done that any surgeon would have been proud to have done it. He was one of my successes with the bare scrotum and now minus his fault was one of the attractions at Kelso that year. He made £400 to R.G.C. Murray of Spittal, and was without a shadow of a doubt the most outstanding sire the breed produced for 30 years. His blood is in every Border Leicester alive today.

One of his descendants, Angus Showwinner, was obtained again by accident. I had selected one of the Spittal sons of the great sheep I have been telling you about — the one and only "Bow Tie." He was No. 7 in Robin's lot. I was bidding for him in the ring when a heavy hand fell on my shoulder and the voice of Ben Wilson, who had come to see how the sale was going, demanded to know how I was keeping. I turned to speak to him and Ian Clark knocked down the tup to somebody else.

I said "Ben, hold it, I was trying to buy a tup just now and I've missed him, but No 9 is very like him so I will buy him instead."

This I did, but did not like him very much and only gave him six ewes. After some days Dougal Cameron my shepherd said, "I'll have to take that Spittal lamb into the buchts to catch him. He is I think even wilder than his father."

I said, "Dougal, we'll give him another six ewes."

One of that six was the mother of the famous Angus Showwinner who almost rivalled his grandfather as a breeder. If it is true that to reach eminence as a breeder of livestock you need skill, it is equally true you need luck. By millions of miles it is the greatest gift, bestowed by providence on some of us and denied to the rest. When we stand beside a litter of pups at six weeks old deliberating which one is to be our constant companion for the next ten years, we may as well just take the blackest one or the biggest one or the smallest one, because it is the one with the most luck we are looking for and there is no way of knowing.

100 YEARS FROM NOW

It was a few days before the new year in 1968, and we were getting a batch of feeding ready for the hill ewes. My grieve Joe Troup always bruised in the evening for at least two reasons. There was no chance of an interruption from a ploughman, reporting his tractor was layered or he had lost a bar point, and it shortened the long winter nights sitting in the house listening to bairns yattering away. As the bruiser hopper held a ton, there was not much to do as long as everything went all right, but you had to be on the alert all the time. You had to adjust the rollers to suit the hardness of the barley, periodically put a drop of oil on the bushes or bearings, and check that the feed remained constant and as anybody who has done it will know most bruisers rattle and vibrate terribly. This night, with everything going sweetly, the two of us were leaning on the feed barrier in the cattle court next door, speaking about whose calf this one was, and how it was thriving better than that one, when Joe said,

"This is one thing that folk will still be doing 100 years from now, the farmer and the grieve speaking in the evening about their cattle and sheep, and next week's work and how forward they are compared with their neighbours. The farmer will be an old kind of chap like you, not that you are old really" — he said — "but you are older than me, I mean, and it's right that I should be younger than you as you are fleet when you're young and the amount of work we do here you have to move yourself. You've heard the saying 'from daylight to dark' ", he added, "We have them beat, for we are from dark to dark."

I could not argue, so I said, "Go on, Joe, tell me more of what the two of them will be talking about waiting on the bruiser a hundred years from now."

"Well," he said, "They will speak about men, the good ones that can work like me, the ones that know about beasts and dogs like you, the useless buggers that don't check their oil levels every morning and get runaways on braes, the lassies that have been nicked and who was getting the blame. When you think about it, they will speak mostly about folk, just the same as we do, but there will be helluva changes in the way they live."

"By jove, Joe, you have it well thought out — could you give me an example or two of the way you think they will live?" I asked, and I had not long to wait.

"Well, as I said, they will be speaking about somebody and the farmer being older as I have said will say 'Aye, it's right enough, he is a good man, my father knew his father — he was married.' The young grieve is puzzled. 'Married you say,' he enquires, 'what does that mean?' 'Well' says the farmer, 'you may find this a bit difficult to believe but 100 years ago lots of people were married. I'll try to tell you what happened. You know down at Kingoldrum where those old gravestones are? That square with the old founds was at that time a building called a Church, and people went there every Sunday to sing and pray to their God. They prayed for health and good harvests, mainly, but also for good Government. Come to think of it,' he reflected, 'they did not have much luck in that line. Anyway, one chap stood up in a box like thing they called a pulpit and led the proceedings, he wore a black frock and had his collar on back to front. He was called a minister. But this married stuff — the minister would announce one Sunday that there was a purpose of marriage between, say, Will Brown and Jean Smith, in three weeks time and would be asking any of them if they could think of any reason for them not being married to let him know as soon as possible. He would say the same the next Sunday so that by the time everybody in the district would have heard about it.

" 'Then on the day of the wedding — that's another name for a marriage — both people concerned would bring all their friends to the church where they would all sit down dressed up to the nines, and listen to the minister speaking to the two. This is more or less what he said. "Will, you are quite sure that it's all right for you to marry Jean? and Jean, does the same apply to you?" If they both said yes the minister would then tell them to say I do to the following promises — "Will", he says, "do you take Jean to be your wedded wife, and do you promise to be good to her?" "I do," says Will.

"The grieve could not take any more. 'For God's sake I'm willing to believe you if I can, but you are having me on now! Never have another woman! the chap must have been off his head if he promised such a thing, but admit it, you are joking.'

" 'I expected you would find this hard to believe,' said the farmer, 'but I'll give you my solemn promise that this actually happened, and if they had bairns they brought them to the Church and christened them, all wrapped up in lace shawls and their friends there again, singing like linties. It was sort of like getting your Union card and the wee souls were thereafter part of the system. They had as you said a different way of doing things in the old days.' "

I came back to reality with a jerk, the dirl of the bruiser told us both that the hopper was empty and it was time to shut the motor off. Joe ran — he seldom walked — to attend to it and I was left reflecting. Statistics newly published were showing that one marriage in four did not last while the last census had made the figure one in nine. The problem of one parent families was exercising the minds of local authorities as was juvenile crime attributable to lack of parental control because both were working. Creche and commune were two words that had began to appear on the newspapers, and I marvelled at Joe's prediction of the way things were going. I was wondering if a British Gaddaffi or Khomeni would emerge and change the course of things when Joe reappeared. "Jim" he says "that's everything finished up, it's raining like hell out there and I'm away to my bed. Young Will will likely come into our bed about eleven o'clock and crack for a minute or two before he falls asleep. I take care not to turn over and smore the little chap because I think he will turn a guid een in a year or two."

HARRY MATTHEWS

Where the road from Blairgowrie meets the Inverness one at Dunkeld is a signpost bearing the easily remembered information: Inverness 100 miles. As I had stopped to ensure the road was clear fter line 9, opposite page:-

And more and further, do you promise never
o have another woman?"
I do" says Will again.
he grieve .....

HARRY MATTHEWS

It was going to be a brave new world, the
aude Report in England was accepted by the
overnment as was the Wheatley one in Scotland.
ocal Government with its outdated and obsolete
ethods was to be replaced by the modern two
ier method where efficiency was to be the
atchword, co-operation between everybody the
ormal and accepted routine and even the poor
ould be pleased. To make sure that the change-
over would go smoothly a two day conference
as held in Inverness, starting at 9.30 a.m. both
ornings. Angus was represented at it by John
ates, County Architect and Planning Officer,
ith two members of his staff, while I as
lanning Chairman attended as an elected
ember. I left Aucharroch at 5 a.m. complete
ith sleeping bag in case nobody wanted me at
ight, and a huge thermos of coffee and some
iscuits as a precaution against possible
amine.

before emerging on to it, I had time to study the distinguished looking and immaculate gentleman standing beside it. On his head was
a bowler hat and in his hand a bulging brief case. I looked at the
car clock; it was 6 a.m. exactly. His look straight at me was not accompanied by any movement, but I instantly recalled the account
of the sword fight in the three Musketeers, when Athos, weak with
wounds, could not with honour ask D'Artagnan for help, but he
could look — so I stopped beside him and asked if I could render
any assistance. He said that if I was going towards or to Inverness
he would be much obliged if I could give him a lift as he meant that
day to call at the office of the H.I.D.B. I said that whatever misfortune had left him stranded at that time of the morning was my good
fortune, for 100 miles with no one to talk to was somewhat dull.
He complimented me on my kindness and got in after carefully putting his case, which I now saw was of finest leather, elaborately carv-
ed, on the back seat. I put the Rover into drive and we moved
smoothly off. My passenger offered no conversation and I know we
were both at the same job, wondering what each other was and how
best to get relaxed together.

I was sure I had picked up some VIP. The polished manners, the
bulging and expensive but well used briefcase gave the impression
of some top civil servant, the faint touch of an accent in his speech
which I could not identify, suggested some time spent abroad, and
I began to think of Ambassadors and Attachés and Newspaper
Editors and 007's and Cabinet Ministers. He sat beside me, relaxed
and assured and I knew he was waiting for me to start.

I began as usual about the weather, was it not a beautiful morning and did he not agree that Scotland in May was quite something.
I scored first go, he enthused about the beauty and majesty of the
Highlands, and admitted that in his travels he had never witnessed
anywhere surpassing them, although certain areas of Canada had
many of the same inspiring features. Canada, I said, had been until
recently regarded by most people as a land of opportunity where
diligence and energy would be amply repaid, but of late there seemed to be some unrest about Frenchmen and Quebec, and talk of
breakaways and managing without Queens. Would he care to up-
date me?

"Well, it's like this," he said "It's going through one of those
phases that's hard to explain. There is plenty of everything but work,
and the young have taken to the roads. They call themselves flower
people and they take over a town for a week or two before moving
on. They live on Government handouts and squat on private property, and although the local authorities would move them on, this
Trudeau won't let them. As the town jailhouse and armoury is
Government property as opposed to Council, he allows them to stay

till they nearly wreck the place. One of the state governers, an acquaintance of mine, is trying to get the law amended so that property owners may claim damages against the Government for loss or injury caused by these mobs.''

The words of Fletcher of Saltoun in the book *Scotland in 1680* came rushing back. ''And in the summer hundreds of these villains roam the hills robbing and demanding food from the people, and living in drunken debauchery. It were better for the nation they be transported.'' Perhaps they had been.

''Is this kind of behaviour common in the States as well?'' I asked, still probing as gently as I could.

''Not really,'' said he, ''The big problem there is colour, as you know, and it's going to take a lot of solving. I think the timescale here is important. The Kennedys are going too fast and the Wallaces too slow. I think it's a mistake to award social relief based on the number of children a woman has, because this means that the low IQ groups have large families, while the intelligent people stop breeding because they cannot afford to bring up their own children because they are bringing up the others via penal taxation. One would have thought they should have learned from the Greeks.''

I thought to myself, ''It can't be very often that a Rolls or a Daimler breaks down in Dunkeld at five in the morning,'' and had another go. Did he think that Europe was settling down to a peaceful coexistence of all its different nations after the two wars? He was hopeful, he said, that the discovery of the atom bomb would be a blessing to mankind in that wars were now too dangerous a way to solve international problems. He had been much impressed, he said, on a recent visit to Austria, by the investment in winter sport facilities, and his family had enjoyed skiing under luxurious conditions, which owing to the foreign exchange rate at the time had rendered their stay relatively inexpensive.

The remaining miles were taken up by a discussion on the relative merits of different religions, and by the time we had agreed that Christianity had a lot in its favour, I had drawn up in a car park just beside the Town Hall. It had been a good run up, it was five minutes past eight. Remarking that the Board Office would not open till nine, my passenger courteously thanked me for bringing him so comfortably to his destination and enquired if as some small gesture of his appreciation, he could at least purchase a cup of coffee for me at a nearby shop which he said appeared to be open. I at once insisted that the pleasure of his company had indeed been more than ample reward, and producing my massive flask said it would be a favour to me if he would share it as I could not possibly consume it all. With a smile he accepted the proffered cup, took a biscuit and we sat reflecting that Thermos had bequeathed to mankind a very useful discovery.

When we had put the empty Thermos flask back in the bag and it was obvious we were about to separate, I said,

"Maybe it is right that we should know each other. My name is Jim Findlay, I am a farmer, and I am up here to attend a conference on local government."

There was a long pause, then he said, "My name is Harry Matthews, I am a hotel manager, I'm broke and I'm up here to try to get a job."

The tears were running down his cheeks. I waited till he got control.

"Harry," I said, "We have half an hour yet, would you like to tell me because maybe I can help..."

Twenty-four years ago he had taken his young wife from their native Glasgow to make their fortune in the catering business in Canada, and by hard work by both had risen over the years to be managers of one of the best hotels in the country, his job being considered in the trade as one of the plums in the well-established company's chain of hotels. By scrupulous saving — but not at the expense of the education of his two sons — he had put both through university — his wife and he had amassed a bit over $50,000 and he was looking for a hotel of his own. When this became known he had been approached by a syndicate and invited to join the company they were forming to run a rival chain of hotels, three of which they had already acquired. The post they were offering was Managing Director, with generous fees for himself and wife and total discretion in the expansion of the company. The prospectus allowed him to invest whatever capital sum he wanted. He had talked it over with his wife, and they had decided to take the plunge. He paid in $50,000 to the company account and longing once more to visit the land of their birth, had used all their money on a four month holiday in Europe.

"That was the time my sons skied in Austria," he said, "Not two years ago yet, and now I couldn't buy them a table tennis bat."

I waited again until he could go on. When they returned after their holiday, the only one they had ever had as a family, they went to take up residence in the largest of the three hotels, but found that much of the furniture was no longer there and the staff had not been paid for some time. He tried to contact his partners to see what was going on, but was unable to trace them. Legal investigations showed that his was the only capital that had been paid in, and had been used in furnishings and wages. The creditors were pressing for the purchase price of the hotels and there were no funds to meet their demands. Only by selling the buildings was he able to meet his liabilities and he was left practically penniless. What with the flower people he had told me about and the political uncertainty at the time, the family had decided to try to make a fresh start in Scotland because they were sure that with the oil boom in the north there would be great opportunity catering for all the single men working the rigs and making platforms. His wife was living at 45 Broxburn Place or Street and he was to see a Mr Scott of H.I.D.B. to discuss what help if any, they would give him to set up in business and start all over again. He stopped and sat quiet, but I could feel his hurt.

"Harry," I said, "I don't care if I never go near my meeting, would you let me come with you?"

The receptionist was polite but formal. Did Mr Matthews have an appointment, because Mr Scott was very busy in the mornings and would he care to say what business he wanted to discuss and would not somebody else do. I said I was sure Mr Matthews would not mind if I told her that I was the Chairman of the Planning Committee of Angus County Council, and that Mr Matthews and I were interested in large scale catering development in the area and that I was certain Mr Scott would see us at once when he knew the nature of our visit. Nor was I in error for in no time we were ushered into the great man's presence. Harry made no bones about it; he repeated to Mr Scott what he had told me, asked if he could lease some suitable building and start up, what grants or loans could be got and how should he go about things. Mr Scott said he would give nim all the relevant pamphlets and, if he would leave his address, would get in touch with him if a suitable building turned up.

I felt things slipping so I went in both feet first, and said I was sure he would not need to get in touch, as Mr Matthews would be seeking employment in the town and would be calling daily to be kept abreast of developments. Harry nodded agreement to this suggestion and with me earnestly imploring Mr Scott to do the limit on Harry's behalf, we took our leave. I asked Harry if he had enough money to get in touch with his wife and to tell her what he was doing. He assured me he had, and with our first and last handclasp I watched him making his way to the Labour Exchange to get started with any job in a hotel.

I made my way back to the Town Hall, apologised to the Chairman for being one hour late and sat down. As far as I was concerned the Conference might well have been in Chinese. I lived again the tragedy I had accidentally stumbled into — the long years' slog day in day out, the gradual increase in the bank balance, the satisfaction of the boys at school, the final realisation of their business ambition, the celebration of the European Holiday, the anguish and loneliness of the crash and its aftermath. The dignified acceptance of fate and the determination to try once again. The speaker said something which made people applaud so I did it to be like the rest.

The new authorities, he said, would be composed of members of political parties working for party ends and a nucleus of non-aligned men and women serving the public interests. Setting aside for the moment the politicians, and many in his profession believed the setting aside should be permanent, officials should concentrate in getting the others into the important posts in local government which strategy would ensure the continuation of fair and unbiased administration. This time I clapped louder than the rest and noted the speaker was the Town Clerk of Inverness. At the conclusion of his speech my own problem was solved. I would not take politics into local government.

At the afternoon meal I made it my business to sit directly opposite this man, and after enquiring about the general prosperity of the city, acquainted him of the circumstances of my late arrival, and asked him to bestir himself in my friend's interest, and to use his influence with Mr Scott of H.I.D.B. so that the Matthews might prosper. He wrote some notes in his diary and promised to help.

The day's business being now ended I wondered where within a radius of 40 miles I would most like to spend the night, and the McGillivrays of Calrossie to whose hospitality I enjoy a constant invitation were an easy winner. From the nearest box I phoned and was rewarded by Di's unmistakable and attractive Australian accent.

"Of course, Jimmie, come on along, but give me an hour to get the big house ready, we have some Americans coming tonight."

Di and Donald were working hard to pay off their father's death duties and the rest of the family's share of his estate, and the Castle was let furnished to the oil tycoons from the new world. Donald had inherited the most famous Shorthorn herd in the world, and was doing his best to keep it that way. The three of us sat late into the night speaking about bulls and tups, dogs and rugby players, droughts in Victoria and soaring land values and wages, how important a good CA was and how on a previous visit I had been impressed by the Planning Officer for Ross & Cromarty named George Peace, how he was insisting that communities stayed as such and did not develop into one huge urban sprawl, and how to allow some degree of flexibility within one predestined and inflexible whole.

"He is a close friend of ours," Donald said, "We often go out together."

I thought of Harry somewhere in Inverness, brief case and all, and related the events of the day urging my friends to interest George Peace in Harry's dilemma, and enlist his active support. I slept without rocking and returned to day two of the Conference with an easy mind.

At the conclusion I proposed a vote of thanks to the organisers, the speakers, our hosts and especially the caterers whose contribution in fact was by far the most important in the success or failure of an exercise of this kind, and for which profession I forecast a glowing future in an area such as theirs with their expanding population and oil related affluence. I ended by suggesting that a search should be made for someone with international experience and expertise in this field so that this industry could expand relative to the others.

Back home again I got into the moleskins, got out Hector and took the hill road.

When I told Nan about what had happened she was not impressed. "You have always been a sucker for a hard luck story, nobody knows that better than me."

Harry, if you ever read this, and if what I did helped you and yours, I would like to meet you once again. If Nan is right and you were having me on, I stand and salute you — you are the most convincing story teller in the business.

A NIGHT AT THE FIRESIDE

It must be wearing on for thirty years since first I met William Rennie Esq, of Berryhill, Kelso, and we all bless the day it happened. As was my wont, and that of my father before me, I had travelled down to Kelso on the second Thursday of September from Perth where I had been selling Blackface rams. The tup sale season is to a Findlay what the word hectic was made to signify. Perth on Thursday, Kelso on Friday, Lanark on Tuesday, Aberdeen the next Tuesday with Caithness, Lockerbie, Newton Stewart plus hosts of minor ones all scrambling to find a free day in the calendar. Our Kelso tups travel to the sale on Wednesday so that they may rest after the journey, and fill themselves up to look their best on sale day. My arrival at the sale field about half past six has always been the first source of news about what the trade had been like at Perth — who got the top price, who paid it, was it a good beast and so on. Naturally my interest was to get news of prospects for the next day and to have a quick look round other people's in order to select the two or three from which I would next day purchase my next stock ram.

Thus engaged, my attention was attracted to a lorry about to unload a consignment. It did not reverse to the pens, but stopped in the open field some fifty yards away. The first thing that emerged was a black and white collie who wasted no time in getting round to the rear where he showed by his demeanour that he wanted the door opened at once. By this time the driver had arrived, not oversized by any means but active and busy. Advising the dog to stand back till he got the door down, our hero lowered the massive wooden door-cum-gangway. This had scarcely touched the ground when the dog ran up it, entered the float and emerged with about a dozen rams, which the two of them proceeded to walk to their pen, at the gate of which the dog took post. I wondered what kind of a cast he had, so I said my herd: "Andrew, let out our tups."

Rejoicing in their unexpected freedom the tups made haste to gain what they thought was the grassiest bit of the sale field where they, after one or two bouts of sparring, started to graze. I approached the man with the dog, informed him of my misfortune of the tups getting away and asked if he would send his dog for them seeing he had him handy. To this request the reply was, "Sure, come bye, Roy," and off he went in a beautiful clockwise circle, from the top of which he approached the grazing tups, and stopped about ten yards in front of them.

"There you are then," said the man. "He will haud them there till you get them."

"Could he not bring them?" I asked. He looked at me more in pity than in anger.

"Listen son. He's more used to dairy cows. He'll bring them if I tell him but I'll no guarantee they will a hae lugs, they maun be used wi gey canny dugs to be grazing up to him that way. I'll come up with you and we'll drove them doon so that there's nae accidents."

"Thank you a lot," I said when the gate was secured. "That's a useful dog you have there, tell me a bit about him."

"His name is Roy," said he, "He's nearly four years old, he's registered and he's not for sale."

"I did not ask if he was for sale," I said.

"No son, I ken you didna" — he looked at me straight in the eye "but that was your next question."

"A mind reader as well," I said and extended my hand. "My name is Jim Findlay."

"Ah ken that fine, you aye have first class sheep." He gripped my hand. "A'm Willie Rennie, frae Berryhill, out at the racecourse."

We have been close friends ever since.

If anybody ever fitted the description of being a character, it is Willie. He might be flying to Helsinki with dogs for Finland, or to Paris to assess the EEC situation, or to the Calgary Stampede to teach the North Americans the virtues of Clydesdales. He might be motoring to Devon where he has heard of a good two year old thoroughbred, or to some hill farm displenish sale where he thinks there might be some harness by some prestige maker. Willie's life is one of continuous whirl, with varied and demanding activity, which brings him into contact with people in every facet of the social structure. He is the chap to get in touch with if no one else can supply you with whatever you want. He can help a Duchess needing a safe pony for her children or a collector needing a replica of the first grain drill used by Jethro Tull. Kept in full vigour by the ample supply of beautifully prepared wholesome farm food served whenever he happens to come home by his talented and understanding wife Nessie, the bold boy, owing to his business contacts, is able to hold forth on national and international affairs with a conviction and force which demolishes all but the most dogmatic of those who have a different view. Closely guarded secrets of bygone generations may be unravelled by a bit of judicious prompting, and theories confirmed or rejected by quoted examples for or against. Nor is he loath to benefit his audience with advice about the stock exchange and which shares are liable to double within a year.

"What makes you think that, Willie?" some potential investor may ask.

"Never you mind that, where I got it is known in the trade as 'reliable sources'."

Now it came to pass that as our friendship deepened, my tups stayed at Berryhill instead of in the sale field on Thursday, having been driven out there by the now self-appointed assistant one year when a rainstorm turned the low-lying sale field into a lake. Because of the facilities available on the farm the move became permanent, and I stayed overnight with my hosts. Will and I would crack into the small hours and Will would bring me up to date on the state of the world. Every year he told me which of the commodities he handled had done him best, and how I could better exploit some asset under my control. Willie had visited Forter the year I under-took the management and was in no doubt as to what should be done. "Buy every garron mare you can get a hold of and cover them with a thoroughbred stallion. By the time the foals are two years old they will be worth a fortune," he said. "This Pat Smythe is never off television and a the rich folk will be wanting ponies for their bairns, there's nae doot aboot it," he added, "Horses will be with us lang after motors have been forgotten about."

"Well, Will," I said next year, "What's the best thing for mak-ing money just now?"

"There's nae doot aboot it," said he, "it's Chihuahua dugs. You have nae bother getting 25 guineas for a pup at six weeks old. You lose some of them at the pupping though as they have been ruined by line breeding. It's a darned shame, you can have a litter of col-lies — good honest collies, and you'll not get a fiver for the lot. There are three things an article needs to make folk keen to buy it, one: it is expensive to produce, two: it is difficult to maintain, and three: it is of no earthly use to anybody. I hope you bought a lot of mares last year when I told you," he added mischievously, "They are about as dear again now."

Next year I put the usual question.

"Jim," he said "I'm nearly ashamed to tell you, it's taken me so long to see it. It is the easiest money I have ever had in my life and nae risk whatever." He paused for the full significance to sink in, then, "I've putten Nessie back to the teachin — she can hae a her work done and my dinner in the oven afore she goes in the fore-noon, and she's back in time to make my tea and do the pigs and hens. Twenty-four pound for five days, and paid on holidays, and apairt from the money it keeps her frae wearying."

We get the pleasure of a visit nowadays for two or three days now that Andrew, their son, is married and living in the farm-house, and if Will wants to wind down a bit; we invite some of our friends to meet them over a dram or a bite of supper, and as readers may suppose the topics are wide and varied.

Jim Robertson and Mary from Braidestone were up one night and Jim was telling us about a recent visit he had paid to Canada — great wheat land, he said.

"Maybe it is noo," said Willie, "but it wasna much use for anything till my great grandfather's cousin Wattie killed off the wild horses."

I knew that this was going to be good, so we asked him to elaborate somewhat.

"Well I canna tell you exactly the year he went out, but it was aboot the time they discovered that meat would keep in a tin — I suppose it might be nearly a hundred years ago. At that time the whole country was covered with scrub and bent grass, nae fences anywhere and if anybody tried to grow anything it got eaten with the wild horses. At last the government saw the damage they were doing and they put Wattie in charge of getting them killed out. Now this was in the days before refrigeration was known about, and as you know" (which we didn't) "horse meat has to be kept in a low temperature. So the first thing Wattie did was to get a slaughterhouse and canning factory combined built right away up in the coldest bit he could find. He built his factory right across the Yukon River and put up a huge corral, hundreds of acres on the south bank. At the same time he hired native drovers and they started to gather up the border with the USA and sweep everything before them heading north. Wattie had them told of course not to hash them, he wanted them all in good order when they came to the corral. It took over a year to drove them to the factory. When the last one was through the gate the drovers followed them in, hauled the bridles off and let their mounts join the rest. Wattie kept them on to help with the killing and canning. Then the wisdom of Wattie's plan was easy seen. Every bit of horse that would not can was dropped through trapdoors into the river and washed out to the sea, keeping the whole thing absolutely clean and hygienic. The killing went on at full speed till the last horse was slaughtered, over three quarters of a million of them. The tinned meat was exported all over the world and they used the money they got for it to put up wages so that they could get Scotsmen to come into the country. They named some of the burns after the new immigrants; you'll hae heard of the Mackenzie River.''

We waited while Will took preventative action to ward off dehydration, then somebody asked, ''What did Wattie do after that?''

''Ah'' said Will, ''He carried oot the second part of his plan. Wi a the blood and guts going down the river half of the fish in the Atlantic were jammed in it frae bank to bank and the other half swimming about the mouth of it waiting to get in. Wattie had known that this would happen and he was ready. He lowered nets from the factory floor and shed off all the fish over a certain size. These were forced to swim up a kind of a lade which again separated them into different sections of the cannery where each fish practically swam into its own tin. As far as I know they are still canning there to this day.''

We marvelled at Wattie's contribution to international well-being. ''They might have renamed the Yukon the Rennie,'' I said at last. ''Did they not mark their appreciation of his genius in any way?''

''They didna get the chance,'' said Will, ''After he saw everything was working fine at the cannery he got homesick and came home and took a croft at Carnwath.''

Next day the Rennies were going home, but just before departing Willie fell in with a *Scottish Farmer Album* of 1913 in my bookcase. He was immediately absorbed and reverently turned page after page with the odd remark about some champion or other. ''Ah,'' he said, ''Here's Dunure Footprint, the greatest stallion there has ever been.''

''I don't know, Willie,'' I said, ''there's some that say his father Baron of Buchlyvie was a better one.''

''Nonsense,'' says Willie, ''he wasna half the horse of Footprint, and what's more he wasna his father, Footprint was really off his own mother's father Auchinflower.''

''That's not what the studbooks say, Will,'' I defended.

''I don't give a damn about the books — my Aunt Lorna's man's brother was Auchenflower's groom. It was him that told us the right way of it. He said that they covered the mare with Baron of Buchlyvie on the Friday afternoon, but it was not a good service so they served her again with Auchenflower on the Monday when she was in full heat.''

''Is there no end to your knowledge, Will?'' said I, ''Seeing your auntie's brother-in-law told you so much about it, did he, by any chance mention the exact time of day on the Monday when they served her with her own father?''

Willie never lifted his eyes from the photo. ''Fower o'clock in the morning,'' he said ''they didna want anybody to ken aboot it. Look after that book,'' he said, ''I'm gonna hae a right read of it next time I am up.''

We may recall that in 1960 Willie forecast that in due course all the rich people would be wanting ponies for their children, but he could have been more explicit and said for their daughters because sons would far rather have MG's. I had been subjected to massive pressure from Sally — then about nine years old — to get her a horse. She had fallen heir to a riding hat and crop that had belonged to her older sister Jane before she changed to dancing for exercise. Being a farmer, some of the reasons for not having a horse did not apply; I could not say we had nowhere to keep it, or hay to feed it, but I did not surrender until I read one of her school essays. It was entitled ''My horse'' and it contained the sentence: ''My bike is my horse, and I go everywhere on it — over to Evelyn's where they have real horses.''

That night I phoned Willie and told him to get a horse for Sally. In due course the said horse arrived after spending a month at Berryhill ridden daily by Willie to make sure he had no vices. He was a four year old dark brown gelding, about 13.2 hands, lean and shaggy and he looked as if butter would not have melted in his mouth. He came complete with saddle and bridle and settled in like a native. Easy to catch and tackle, he transported his new owner and her friends as well through the fields to begin with, and soon on roads as well. Now an essay would read ''I have a horse and I go everywhere on it — over to Evelyn's to see its friends.'' Dave had however the usual snags that horses introduce on a stock farm. His field was shared by the milk cow, so of course you could not leave the gate open to get her into the byre in case Dave got out and made for the cornroom. He had his kind's habit of having the odd chase among a flock of sheep being penned, which activity attracted retaliation by people whose dogs were winded by getting the sheep that far, in the form of a stone thrown accompanied by bad language.

We were all prepared however to put up with these minor troubles, for Dave was the magnet for the affection and care of all the children on the farm, and when they were with him we knew what they were up to. A new sleekness had now appeared on the summer coat and the girth needed out a hole or two. Dave was having it good, and could often be seen galloping and snorting up and down or having a chase of the cow to work off some energy. A new game was developing called ''scrape you off''. The rules were bareback and no bridle. You leaned against a gate when you saw your mistress coming home from school and enticed her on to your back. You then set off at a slow trot to where a tree grew alongside a wall with just enough room for you to squeeze through, which you did with the object of leaving your rider de-horsed. The rider of course had to try to stay up and this could be achieved by lying straight across your back until you had passed through the obstacle. If you managed to dislodge her you stopped at once and braced yourself so that she could remount with a running leap when you would repeat the process either till her mother shouted her for her tea or till you were fed up and would not do it again. Although I had an uneasy feeling that I should not allow this sort of stuff, I did nothing about it and gradually the game became more sophisticated, with sudden acceleration, quick turns, crash stops, the lot, but still I did not see what was happening for I so far had not observed anything wrong when he was bridled.

I suppose the first real disaster happened one day when the pig escaped from its sty which, like the henhouse, was in the cow park. Dave went berserk, cleared the fence like Red Rum and did not stop running till he reached a copse halfway up the hill where he stood snorting and steaming like a newly made dung midden on a frosty morning. He looked completely different from the pony I had known. He was only caught with difficulty and had practically to be levered back into his field where he ran snorting, tail straight out back and forward along the fence farthest from the pig's cray. To calm him down we shifted the pig to a cray in the steading, and peace was restored.

The next episode was when I shot a pigeon which was contemplating, from what it thought was a safe place, the pros and cons of a diet of fresh vegetables out of our garden. At the bang of the gun Dave again cleared the fence and made for the hill where the identical procedure was needed to get him back as on the last occasion.

Worse was to follow. I had an acre or two of marshy land at the bottom of the field next to the cowpark where you could knock down a hare or a duck or a pheasant at short notice if the occasion demanded, and this day I killed a fine cock flying towards the steading. Dave in full gallop already from the shot was further maddened if possible, by the bird crashing alongside him as he ran. He cleared a 5'6'' gate from the low side, landed on the farm road and set off for the glens. By the time I got the Landrover and set off in pursuit, he was out of sight. I made up on him four miles away relating his experiences to two new formed acquaintances, whom he had invited down to the roadside to meet him. As I approached with the halter, uttering soothing phrases like, "Man, Dave, you are a grand chap, and a braw jumper but we'll have to get away home now, it will soon be teatime.'' I saw for the first time that he held me responsible for his spookings, because whenever I got within ten yards he was ready to take off again so I had to await somebody else coming. In a few minutes Norman Ogg turned up in his Landrover, took the halter, and caught him without any bother. Anger welled up in me for I had put up with a lot. I wondered what the next event would be which he would classify as spookable, a window reflecting the sun maybe, a fox crossing his park to have a look at the burn bank, a field roller on the metal road en route for a field — the possibilities were unending. I could have seen David Broome and Co. in hell. Fortunately the halter was a strong one so I tied the end to the towbar of the Landrover and set off, dragging the protesting Dave, skidding along the road. He did not continue arguing about things for very many yards however; he had cast two shoes somewhere and he discovered it was much less painful to run than to be dragged. I returned him to his field and gave instructions — no more corn.

For a while things went fine, he behaved all right with the children although I put the public road out of bounds in case. I kept out of the way when he was being ridden, for he treated me with open suspicion. Although I did not know it a new trick was being perfected. When your rider wanted you to turn by reining, you just turned your head round into your ribs and stood still. If she tried to get you to move by digging you with her heels, you bit her feet, which discouraged her from persisting to try to get you to proceed in any direction except the one you wanted to go. It was when Willie Rennie came up for a day or two and saw the carry on that the thing finally boiled over. He stared in disbelief as Sally vainly tried to persuade her mount to answer to rein or heel. He slowly pulled off his jacket. I noticed he wore the old spring bands on his biceps to regulate how far down the wrists the shirt sleeves came. His voice came, low and controlled: "Come down a mennit, hen, and gie me a shot."

I gave him a leg up and he touched Dave with his left heel. With the associated tail flick the unsuspecting maverick turned round to bite the offending object but received the full weight of Willie's No. 7's right in the teeth. With a startled leap he bolted up the road but there he got his second cheat. His rider was sitting like a limpet instead of trying to stop him and dug him savagely in the guts every time he slackened speed, until after about ten times round the steading an exhausted Dave was reined up in front of us. This time he moved off beautifully at the first touch, was walked round, then trotted round then once more galloped round. "Now," asked Willie, "where do you keep the pig?" and proceeded to ride right up to the door of the sty where he forced the mastered horse to put his head over the top of the half open door. He returned to the rest of us at the house and dismounted.

"Sally," he said "he's a good horse, but you must keep the better of him — he is in good form — remember there's two ways. Make him fat so he is lazy or make him thin so he is weak."

Sally mounted and moved off, but not before hearing Willie's instructions to me.

"Jim, what's the use of me hunting the Borders and the north of England as well to get a real good horse for you if you are to let him get over her like that. If ever you see him at it just give him ten minutes of what he got from me and knock the bloody nonsense out of him."

About three weeks later one Sunday morning I came down from the hill at about 10 o'clock. Sally was standing at the back door brushing her horse although he was saddled.

"Well, Sal," I said, "what's doing today?"
"Dave was biting my boot again, Dad — you will have to give him a lesson."

I had not been on a horse for 40 odd years, and I had a feeling that there could be problems. He did not like me, the stirrups were short, and the tarmac road looked very hard. I feared he would throw me a time or two until I mastered him but I could not chicken in front of the child. I took a long rein and tied the end round my waist and the other to the bridle, led him down to a stubble field which I thought looked more inviting to fall on, stood him alongside the dyke and levered myself up. With about four bucks, a rear leg standup during which I slipped back, and then a mighty heave of the rump, he threw me over his head to land on my bum about ten yards in front of him. He jumped over me at full gallop and the rope round my waist jerked tight, the headband of the bridle broke and was left sitting with a bridle with no horse in it. I had been pulled about a yard with the jerk of the rope and I looked round to where I had landed for I had been conscious of a sort of crunching feeling on impact, and half expected to see that I had broken the eggs of a deserted pheasant's nest, but there was nothing to be seen. I told the dogs, the three-legged Steve and his mother Pat to "Haud on". I had the idea of tiring Dave out a bit before I remounted so I lit a cigarette and directed the chase. In retrospect that is what I should have done at the start, for after ten minutes or so of Pat at his rear he was pretty well done in and when I told the dogs to let up, he was quite pleased to stand at the gate, head down, blowing like a grampus.

"I'll manage you this time," I thought, and started to rise, but I could not; my legs would not bear my weight and I could not get further than my knees. I thought, "I've sat too long, I've got stiff, or something has got jammed, but if I can get to the dyke and pull myself up with my hands it will go back into place." I pulled myself to the dykeside, and managed to stand up. I was a bit dizzy but I let go of the top of the dyke. When the weight went on my feet, a sickening pain knifed through my back and I fell in a heap. I felt myself getting drowsy.

I was wakened by the sound of people speaking and opened my eyes to see Sally and her mother, the ploughman Alan Low and his wife, and Doctor Finlay McKenzie from Kirriemuir.

"Any idea of your blood group?" asked the doctor and I noticed he was holding a bottle in his hand with a plastic lead from it. I followed it down and saw it connected to a needle stuck into the back of my hand.

"No idea," I said, "but there are plenty of you here, now give me a hand up."

"No, no," said Finlay, "just be still, we are waiting for an ambulance to take you to the infirmary so we can find out what you have done to yourself."

Seeing there was no arguing, I gave up and fell asleep again. This time I was awakened by the ambulance chaps getting a stretcher under me (a very skilled operation) for Finlay forbade me to move a muscle but in a few minutes we set off for Dundee, me lying face down hand out in front, complete with plasma bottle still held by the Doctor, and my wife sitting looking at me pale as a sheet. I turned my head so I could see out of the opposite window, and I thought "Queer how I never noticed before how wondrously beautiful the leaves are at this time of year, maybe its the angle I am looking at them, and of course its Glenogilvie we are going through and it's a beautiful glen at any time." I was too lazy to think about it for I was getting sleepy again ...

... I was back at Marcus Mill, and it was harvest. Dave Milne was on the binder with Tam Star and Rose. It was really hot and I saw the sweat was running down the inside of the horses' legs, when he stopped to put in a ball of twine. I was there with my stick to kill the rabbits. I had on my new sandals to help me to run faster. My father and Davie Andrews the cattleman were stooking and McDougall the gamie, standing at the side of the wood with his gun. I was in great form. Between me and my father's collie Ned, there was no escape for bunny. As I overtook my victims they squeaked in the way they do when they know it's curtains ...

I returned to reality to find we had arrived at Dundee, and I listened with a detached interest to Dr McKenzie discussing my case with the on-duty casualty ward GP. "Lying unconscious in a field — no pulse — gave him bottle — blacking out — no legs, fell off horse, vomiting, no pain."

I was anxious to hear what the new man's verdict would be. My greaser which I had been wearing had been taken off and was lying across the bottom of the stretcher.

"Give me my fags, Fin, I'm dying for a smoke."

The other doctor spoke up. "We are going to have you X-rayed," he said, "I would prefer if you did not smoke till we have a look at the plates."

Half an hour later I watched as the two examined the pictures.

"Little wonder he did not have a pulse when you got him," said the hospital man. "Look at that, his pelvis is broken in three places. It's a blessing you put him on a drip. You have done a good job. We will look after him now; I'll have a blow up of these plates and decide whether to pin him or put him in traction."

"Well Jim," said Dr McKenzie, "I'll get a lift home with your grieve; he has come in to hear what you want done till you come home."

I was taken up to Ward 14 of Dundee Royal Infirmary and put into a bed whose brass plate on the wall declared it had been gifted by so and so in memory of his two sons missing, presumed killed, at Dunkirk. The ward sister was helping to transfer me from stretcher to bed, and I was thinking that her perfume was wasting its time in the condition I was in. As she was taking off my socks and trousers my left leg fell over the side of the bed and I could not do anything about it. As she lifted it back on I got the same blinding pain as I had when I let go the dyke, but this time I knew it was the bones jarring at the breaks, and I screamed involuntary. If ever I had to get a suspect to talk and he had a broken pelvis I would threaten to move one of his legs and I would get the whole shooting match. The sister was not amused.

"Don't shout like that," she ordered, "You will frighten other patients."

"I'll promise," I said, "as long as you don't touch my legs." It was neither the time nor the place; I was suspended by a sling round my buttocks which forbade any movement of the affected areas, and there I lay for three weeks on my back, unable to move anything but my hands.

It was there that I got to know one of the bravest men it has been my good fortune to meet. An ex-cavalry soldier, Paddy, now a doorman at the University, had been grievously wounded by shrapnel and his wounds refused to stay healed. He had had bone grafts and metal pin supports in both legs and arms and the muscle wastage and deformities of his sinews were appalling to see. In spite of all this, Pat was the life and soul of the ward and it was a second home to him; he joked to all and sundry, and was easily the best mannered chap to the nurses. He was an absolute example to the rest of us who were mostly accident victims from car smashes, or steeplejacks who failed to secure their ladders, or football supporters debating the relative merits of a certain Mr J. Stein and a Mr A. McLeod. Directly across the ward from me lay a patient who as well as Pat displayed remarkable resilience in the face of heavy odds. One of his legs had gone wrong and his foot was taken off. The trouble was not arrested so again there was an amputation, this time below the knee. Shortly after I was admitted a further operation was deemed necessary, this time above the knee. He had been, as well as a general labourer, a professional footballer in his youth and talked with personal knowledge of some of the great men of the past with whom he had played. Eck Troup of Forfar, Dundee, Everton, Dundee, Forfar; Eck's wheel had turned full circle. J.B. McAlpine of Queen's Park and his team mate Jimmie Crawford, Dyken Nicol of Dundee who, he said, repeatedly fouled the great R.S. McColl. When McColl had protested at the treatment he was getting and asked the Dyken: "Do you think you are playing football?" he was answered, " No, I don't; my job is to prevent you from doing it."

I used to get the nurses to wheel my bed over beside him so he could tell me more and more of the stories of Dundee of yesteryear. Things went by nines in his house, he said; his mother had nine children, nine hens, nine cats and nine pounds in the tea caddy. The children did a milk round every morning but he, John, being the oldest boy, did the shopping on a Saturday night. With his nine pence he had to get bread, vegetables and beef. The woman in the greengrocers was huge, John said, and when you wanted half a turnip, she would hold it against her tummy with one hand and cut it through the middle with a great big gully. "I used to be terrified when she was doing it," John said, "in case the gully slipped — what a heap of puddings there would have been on the floor." Then, it was best to be the last customer at the butchers because his order was a pennyworth of cuttings. These, John said, were the parts that wealthy customers had asked the butcher to cut off their selected joint — trimmings they are called nowadays — and if you just got in when he was closing he sometimes gave you a whole basinful for your penny and you could keep the family in broth for a week. The carters from the docks to the jute mills, he said, got their whisky a farthing cheaper by showing their whips, and another privilege they enjoyed was the right to urinate against their wagon wheel in the street.

I phoned to Lord Tayside who had a say in the running of Grampian Television and pleaded with him to record a series of John's reminiscences, but David was not a well man and did not take me on. It could well be that it could be done yet though, because John's third operation was successful and he left ward fourteen to go to the limb fitting centre before I was discharged. John, if you read this, I would dearly love to get in touch; although you had nine more get well cards than I had, I am not a bit jealous and my life has been enriched for knowing you.

In case readers get the impression we were all good people in the ward, I have to mention Willie Adams. Willie was another who got a leg taken off but this time it was at the thigh by a double decker bus that he had fallen in front of on a drunken Saturday night brawl. He was as objectionable as Pat and John were admirable; every second word was a curse, he was forever needing attention or demanding the phone, his bedside radio was on full blast — in fact you would have thought he was trying to find out how much the rest of us and the staff would take. He told us he was the baddest man in Scotland, and had been in all the roughest jails, including Inverness where a certain block is pure hell, and you could get neither women or drink for months. "That's the two things I live for," he said, "and I'll do anything to get plenty of both." Nor was he boasting, for daily he was visited by a shapely redhead and demanded screens put all round his bed so he could enjoy privacy on her visits. Incoming calls from his group leaders from phone boxes were a nightly feature. They were gang progress reports or were asking for further instructions as to what or where to rob or slash. As an instance of his arrogance, one night when the sister was doing her 10 o'clock round asking the usual: "Do you want anything to help you sleep, or to relieve the pain" he shocked us all.

"Too right, sister, I want you and I want you bad, haul off your breeks and get in beside me."

"Mr Adams," said the indignant woman, "that is absolutely disgraceful, and I am not to have it. One more word like that and I will send for the doctor to come to you!"

"For Christ's sake, sister, don't do that," replied her insulter, "I'm no a bloody homosexual."

I pressed my emergency bell and demanded to see the matron, told her what had occurred and demanded that Adams be removed forthwith and either put in solitary or flung in the Tay. The matron told him he was on his last chance, just one more fault and he would be out. The muttered imprecations on her departure were loathsome to listen to, but at least they were muttered ones and the radio had been removed. Next day the doctor was doing his round.

"Well, Mr. Adams, I hear you didn't have all that good a night, how are things today?"

"Hellish altogether doctor, a bloody half-wit up there thinks he can bully me, but he'll find out different when we get him outside, is there any chance of getting him shifted out of here before he drives me bloody mad?"

I looked at Pat in the next bed with his wasted leg in traction to try to get the latest graft to take and he put his index finger on his temple in a gesture we all understood. As soon as I was allowed to walk I went down to have a closer look and to get our places in the herd established. His manners had improved with his convalescence, his good-looking face was adorned by a smart moustache but spoilt by a network of scars of various lengths and widths. It is wonderful what disability does to establish a feeling of belonging, and in a few days I included him in my list of people whom my regained mobility enabled me to visit. His language stayed the same, abominably — it was the only way he could communicate and the rest of us accepted the inevitable. He told me he was thinking of going straight, he had the offer of a night watchman's job at a big factory. He would earn £38 a week for himself and his Alsatian dog, and though that was no bloody good he could flog enough for himself to make a decent living. It would still pay the owners over the back to have him, for he would put it out of bounds to the gangs.

A few days before Christmas, and with two sticks to assist my still uncertain legs, I was let home to make room for the usual festive season's orgy of accidents. The young doctor who admitted me was there to see me off.

"Doctor," I told him. "Out of misfortune has come good. I've lasted six weeks without a smoke, since you would not give me my fags, and I made up my mind never to smoke again. There's worse things than a broken pelvis."

"I could have stopped you a lot cheaper if I had known that was the object," was his riposte, "a couple of broken ribs would do the job equally well."

I heard later that Willie Adams had fallen in front of another vehicle but this time with his head. I imagine there are more brothels in hell than in heaven, and I hope for his sake that that is where he is. I am not sure that Old Nick will share my sentiments though, for I bet Willie has given him some sleepless nights.

A LITTLE KNOWLEDGE IS A DESIRABLE THING

I make no apology for the above heading, for if I had no knowledge I would be nothing, yet a lifetime is too short for anyone ever to say "I have a lot of knowledge." Some of us read more books than others, some master more crafts than others, some speak more languages than others or play more musical instruments, some can foretell the weather better than others, and on and on; what I am trying to prove is how incomplete each one of us is. In my own case what time I devote to learning is pretty well confined to reading about the Pharoahs, the Romans, the Greeks and the Gaels, and the contributions to mankind of Werner von Braun and Frank Whittle, Marconi and Baird will forever remain a mystery in my brain. If I had the impudence to guess to which of the great ones I bore even the slightest resemblance I would have to go for Gibran. "To work is to keep pace with the soul of the earth." This always seems to me to have said it all. When I listen to Malcolm Muggeridge or Dr Bronowski, a sense of awe and shame for my abysmal ignorance comes over me, and I take refuge in the old shepherd's assessment of values on being introduced to a famous author: "Ony sauchle o' a body could write a book — but it takes a man to herd the Merrick."

So even as work itself has been to me a near fulfilment, the pleasure of it was instilled in me by caring and ambitious parents whose energies were directed to ensuring that when I grew up I would be able to take my place in the generations of Findlays that knew about the earth and the animals. The book in our house which came at least equal to the Bible was the poetical works of Robert Burns, and nightly in the winter my father would read selected poems from it — all calculated to indoctrinate me to love and respect animals. The poet's greeting to his old mare: "A guid new year I wish thee Maggie" — in our book there was a painting on the page of Burns going up beside her in her stall with a sheaf of oats under his arm and her looking round at him. This was always good to make me sure that my dad was a man like him and if ever I had horses I would be kind to them as well. I periodically sympathised with the unfortunate mouse that got its nest ploughed up but I have ploughed up hundreds of them since. Generally some great brute of a seagull eliminated their problems and even the farmyard hens counted young mice a delicacy and used always to be at the threshing of a stack nabbing them as opportunity offered. I was on the hens' side at this job — trying to fork sheaves with every second string cut does nothing for one's placidity.

The Twa Dogs was another story that left a deep impression — I always grudged Caesar his position of privilege and thought that if I was Luath I could not have gone hunting with him. Yet I knew it wasn't the dog's blame — he could not help who owned him, so it was all right to fraternize (Dogs evidently raked in Burn's day as well.) If my father knew which page "To a wounded hare" was on he never opened it and now I know why — he had had too many acres of turnips ruined with the sods. If they would eat one turnip nobody would grudge them it, but to take one bite out of every turnip in the field so that the first night's frost destroys them is a habit which is quite unpardonable, and hares deserve what is coming to them. Burns' sympathy for the rascals informs us that he either never grew turnips, or that he had them either sheuched or pitted by mid-October.

The poem which was read every time the book was open though, and the one which made the most impression on me — I have been able to say it for over sixty years — is naturally, as one would expect in a sheep breeder's home, "The Death and Dying of Poor Mailie" — the author's only pet ewe — rendered so soulfully by my father, that I always cried at my inability to have been born earlier so I could have run and cut the string that couped her, and helped her up and saved her life. I hoped against hope that there was another verse somewhere in the book, which said that just before she died her master came along and saved her.

"Oh lass, that was a gey near thing,
You're right, I'll burn this cursed string,
And free fae ony irksome tether
You and your lambs will roam together."

Alas, the ending was always the same.

— "Thus said, poor Mailie turned her head,
And closed her een amang the dead."

Surely to the young Scottish stocksman this poem will leave a lifetime impression, and he will be the better person for knowing it — even as the young Roman must have been inspired by Virgil's unforgettable and eternal message: "Others may mould the breathing bronze more delicately or carve living images from marble. Others may plead causes more eloquently, measure the radius of the heavens with a rod, or foretell the rising of the stars. Thou Roman — forget not to govern the nations under thy sway — these shall be thy arts — to crown peace with law, to spare the vanquished, and to humble the proud." When he delivered this immortal tribute to the young Marcellus at his tragic funeral at the age of fourteen, it is little wonder that the boy's mother Octavia swooned with emotion. What a blessing that the Frenchman Champallion found the key to the translation of the hieroglyphics, otherwise no one would have known that which Mer En Ptah instructed to be written of him: "I was husband to the widow, father to the fatherless, but specially kind to him who had no mother. Nobody was hungry in my time and a woman could walk abroad without being molested." What a message for the rulers of today, although I admit that if our present leader got her way we might at least get the last bit right.

I was at a Burns Supper last week and heard the best Immortal Memory I have ever heard. Dr Purdie said that nearly all the Scottish soldiers killed at Balaclava had a book of Burns, with the most fingered page "Scots Wha Hae," which evidently psyched them up to perform deeds of heroism for their native land. It surprises me that Burns fell for this trick, used by kings, dictators and all sorts of human butchers over the centuries to get the common people to kill each other in order to satisfy their own power lust. Perhaps I will grant you Wallace, but Bruce, although he is supposed to be an ancestor of mine, was just a fourteenth century racketeer.

The book the wanderer should carry is *Hamewith*. What a blessing knowledge is, so that we can read *The Alien*, and love our native land for the right reasons.

"For all the time the heather blooms on distant Bennachie
and wrapt in peace the sheltered valley lies
I want to wade through bracken in a glen across the sea
I want to see the peat reek rise."

Or live again the times of country folk, less than a century ago — as depicted as effectively as News of the Week on any television. "A waught of ale to slough his drouth — a pinch to clear his head, and the news came from the Packman like the water down the lade." As a boy how often have I accompanied my father to open the sluice on the Noran to let the water down the lade so we could have a thresh or even to let the lade fill with sea trout in early evening; you can then shut off the water and help yourself. I have seen the tub my mother used for a sink — we had no water in the house except what came from the well in the garden — full of the beauties. Back to the Packman's lade and the sheer descriptive power of the phrase — I used to run alongside the surging column of free energy that powered practically every threshing and grinding mill in North East Scotland. Our forebears' skill in coaxing water round hillsides and often apparently up gradients on the side of embankments clearly demonstrated that they were hesitant to accept Newton's theory about gravity. I used to get a strong feeling that it was faith that got the water to the mill. If you need proof, visit Craigendowie over in Lethnot where there must still be traces of the lade taken up from the Callater Water. Perhaps it does not compare in scale with the first recorded water diversion 5000 years ago when Menes re-routed the Nile round Memphis. Historians credit him for introducing large scale irrigation to the world and very likely this was the object of the exercise — on the other hand maybe he was just needing a weekly thresh. Like most good parents too, the Packman did his best for his family, one a minister, one a lawyer and a skilled one too if we believe the chronicler —

"The second one took up the law and better fit there's few
at chargin sax and eight pence or at keeping gaun a plea
or stirring strife mung decent folk wha left alone would gree."
The youngest of course was a doctor, and according to the story, gey fond of a dram.

Surely the ability to communicate by the written word is the greatest of all human achievements, because each generation can add its contribution to the already known and recorded mass of discovery and invention. I suppose that when Archimedes was mopping up the bathroom floor before his wife could give him a flyteing he must have said to himself, "I'd better write this down, not to fill that bath right up because every time I get into it, it runs over and there's hell to pay."

The first chap who tried to heat up the water by taking in the electric fire with him did not record his important discovery — that was left for his next of kin.

The last observation I would make on the gathering of knowledge is the importance of the teacher, especially his or her ability to present the subject in a way that makes the student long for the next lesson. My idol teacher is called Adam McLure; he taught French in the Morgan Academy when I attended fifty-four years ago. Perhaps I was one of his favourites, I do not know, but I really worked hard to try to please him. On the Education Committee this year, we were debating the banning of the strap — which I hope we never do — and in the lounge later I was instancing teachers who need the belt and teachers who do not, and said I could not remember McLure ever using his. Our Chairman, Dr. W.K. Fitzgerald said that he knew him, and that he was a great bee keeper, and lived in Longforgan. A wave of nostalgia came over me — how I longed to see and hear him once again.

"Mon petit Findlay, dis-moi; pourquoi Charlemagne restait-il la tête baissée?"

I tried — greatly daringly — "Monsieur, parce qu'il voulait admirer sa barbe."

"Are you Mr McLure who taught languages in the Morgan in 1930?" I asked, and was answered in the affirmative. It was as I have said fifty-four years since I had last spoken to or met him, so I thought I'd better introduce myself.

"Mr McLure," I said "you won't know who I am, but I was one of your pupils in 1928 and 1929. My name is James Findlay and I used to travel in every day from Newtyle in the train and I had to get away ten minutes early at night to catch the train home, but I don't expect you to remember me."

"Remember you," came back over the phone, "I recognise your voice." I went to see him next day — we are pals again.

JESS

I wonder if all of us get as involved with events as I do, or if anyone can offer an explanation of the following.

Jim Pearson's young bitch Jess, the grand-daughter of Wiston Cap, was coming to her time to Fred; in fact Nan and I were counting the days — 63 of course — and wondering how many she would have. Six were already spoken for, Jim was wanting two for customers of his own, my son Marcus who will come good with dogs later on, is getting one, Sandy Douglas of Woodhead, who got his last son of Fred killed, Bill Mathers, whose old Hector died this year, and Bert Grant, who is making such a good job of Glendamff.

If I have done any good on Tayside Regional Council it has been my success in getting a no farms amalgamation policy approved; we have several farms in the water catchment areas and we are putting young families into every one as it comes to let. Tayside and Scotland has our excellent Euro-MP Jim Provan to thank for helping me with this when he was a colleague of mine in local government. It maddens me to see hill farms lying unoccupied — where are the Burns, Flemings, Watts, Bakewells, Watsons, Murrays and Mackies of the future to come from? You cannot breed them in cities.

Anyway we decided the pups would be born in four days time and went off to bed. I had had an infestation of rats into the steading and was trapping and baiting them, so the first thing I did in the morning was quickly to let Fred in, then switch on the light, and he usually killed one before they got in among the hay. This morning in pitch darkness I let him in and I heard him dashing about, but, damn me, I could not find the light switch. At last I got it and the place was lit as bright as day. There was no sign of Fred, but lying against the wall on the bare concrete floor was the first Jess I ever owned — in about 1936 — we bought her from Alistair Craig of Pirnmill, Arran, after being captivated by her mother's performance at a trial. Even more astonishing, she was nursing three pups exactly like herself with white flecks dotted here and there on their bodies. On my entry Jess rose, came over to me, and then trotted out of the door and for some reason the sun was shining out of a blue sky. I thought with horror — "God, I haven't been here for two days, and she cannot have had a drink. She will be away down to the burn; now is my chance to drown these pups when she is away." I picked up two of them and put them into a bag and was reaching for the last one when I relented.

"I'll leave you for your mother's sake," I told it, "You're lucky you were furthest away."

I had a bath full of water just outside so I put in a stone, tied the neck of the bag and dropped it in. In a few seconds the bubbles stopped so I went back into the shed. I was standing looking at the survivor wondering who its father could be when it looked up and its eyes were open. "What have you done with Fred and Jess?" it asked. I did not panic; I have trained myself not to under any circumstances. I just stood there looking, wondering if I had heard right. I was not left long in doubt.

"I hope you have not done them any harm, for there would be nobody for me to play with," the little chap pleaded. I wanted to run outside and try to save them but I had waited till the bubbles stopped and I knew it was no use, so I just stood there lost for words feeling like the murderer I was.

The pup crawled nearer and looked me fair in the eye. "We are clever pups you ken," it said, "Would you like to see me bringing you that wheel?"

I turned to where it was looking; on the floor beside some bags of best pulp lay the depth wheel of an Oliver 110A horse plough, about 7" diameter, iron and some seven or eight pounds weight. For the first time I found words.

"Naw," I said, "you could never do that, it's about ten times your weight."

"We'll see then," quoth the pup, "Just watch."

It made its way over to the wheel and I noticed it left a wet trail on the floor like a snail leaves on a flagstone, as it half crawled, half walked, and I thought, "You will damage your navel on that rough concrete," but it reached the wheel in no time. It immediately got its mouth under the rim, and with a herculean effort managed to lever it upright. The rest was was easy — it simply rolled it to me pushing it along with its shoulder in the manner of a school boy shoving his gird. It rolled it right up against my boot and then sat back, eyes now fully open and goodness gracious they were blue.

"What do you think of me now?" it asked.

I considered long before I answered. "You must be the cleverest pup that's ever been born," I told it, "You are not two days old, but you are seeing, you are retrieving, and you are actually speaking — if somebody told me I would think they were mad. What is your name anyway?"

"My name is Ben and you are wrong about one thing," the wee fellow told me, "I'm not the cleverest — actually I am the stupidest of the family, little Jess my sister passed her A-levels in French and German and mother's putting her to university."

It gradually got dark in the shed so I reached up to switch on the light again. This time I got it first go and I looked at my wrist watch which I wear all night to see what time it was. It was quarter to six, and I thought, "It will not be light for an hour yet, but I'd better waken Nan in case we sleep in." She looked across.

"You must have too many clothes on your bed," she said, "You are soaking of sweat. Are you feeling all right?"

"Not really," I answered, "I'm feeling hellish."

She sat up alarmed. "Goodness man, what have you been doing?" she asked.

"I've drowned two of the best pups there have ever been," I said "I doubt I've gone out of my mind."

When I came home at dinnertime she had been into the town for messages, and had met one of her friends, Tib Bishop from Nether Ascreavie.

"You will never guess what she told me," she offered, "Jim Pearson's bitch had seven pups last night, four dogs and three bitches — they are four days early. Jim told my Jim that some job he was on had turned out to be much harder than he thought it would be and the exertion had triggered her early —in fact the first was born in the back of the Landrover. He had got it lying beside the spare wheel."

Sally and I were up to them last Sunday, and a fine litter they are, all doing well. The first one was just beginning to open his eyes — he has a white face with a wide black brow. Jim picked him up and gave him to Sally to hold and she was cuddling the wee morsel and letting him know how lovely he was. I was watching the bitch, and although she was looking there was no hostility in her expression.

"Her nature is right anyway, Jim," I said, "I've seen bitches that would not let a stranger take up any of her pups."

"All her kind are good natured," Jim answered "and anyway she knows that none of us would ever harm her pups."

Sally returned him to his bed and he started sucking like the rest. It was a lovely sight — they were clean, they were dry, they were warm, they were full, and they had one another to play with.

A MAN'S GOT TO DO

Without looking up old records I am going to plump for 1954, but it might be a year either way, when I was asked to judge the sheep at the Orkney County Show. This is the show where all the champions of the smaller shows compete and I suppose is the most important day in the year in normal circumstances. However, since World War Two the most important day is now when the biggest American warship pays a visit during some NATO Naval Exercise with hundreds, even better, thousands of sailors and GI's all hungry to get their feet on terra firma for a day or two. That is when the natives compensate for months of isolation from the outside world, and the shops of Kirkwall will do more in a day than is usual in a month. If the price tickets in the shops are not the same as the day before who is anyone to criticise; a wreck blown up on the coast of an island is one of the perks of the natives, and how much better than a wreck is a ship with loads of crew who have two month's pay to get rid of.

But back to my visit — the show committee, evidently determined to be regarded as the ultimate in hosts, had laid on a conducted tour of the island for about thirty judges with their wives, to let us see the last inhabited one-roomed house with the fireplace in the middle, and the sleeping quarters round the wall. The bus I was in was for the men — the women had one of their own. I suppose this arrangement was made by some experienced organiser who knew that a group of livestock breeders in various stages of sobriety were liable to use language or conduct conversations likely to cause acute embarrassment to such a genteel company as each one's wife wanted the rest to believe her to be. When we came to Maes Howe our guide told us about the three levels depicting different ages of occupation, for longer than 3,000 years, and how the excavators were finding necklaces of that age made from sheep's teeth. Phrases like "Well I'll be buggered" or "In the name of Jesus" were evidence of our wonder and amazement as the secrets of the long ago were revealed to our incredulous minds. When Scara Brae and the Churchill barriers were inspected we knew we had witnessed a bit of both ends of the turbulent history of the land which eventually became a part of us through the marriage of a Viking princess to a Scottish King, Malcolm and Margaret, if memory serves me well.

Our last visit was to be to a Nissen-type hut which had been the abode of some Italian prisoners during the War and which they had converted into a place of worship with evidently a very skillfully painted Nativity Scene painted in colour on the inside of the end window above the home-made pulpit. We dutifully dismounted from our bus and followed our guide through the door, as usual cracking amongst ourselves about some of yesterday's exhibits and could it be possible that the natives drank like this all the time. As we crossed the threshold an astonishing thing happened. Suddenly the place was absolutely quiet, and those who wore caps removed them in an atmosphere of compelling and awesome reverence. When our guide in hushed tones began to tell us how this plain iron prison had been transformed into this shrine using such materials as they could get, from broken fence posts to derelict farm implements, the dimly lit interior seemed to glow from some supernatural force. At the end of the description I had to make a conscious effort to make my way to the door and re-enter the world of the present. This time nobody had anything to say; we all stood quiet each with his own thoughts. After a little I walked round the outside and noticed for the first time a collection box with its invitation for subscriptions to maintain the building, but it seemed that familiarity had done its stuff and the lock had been broken.

I could not get peace all evening and night. I felt as Howard Carter must have felt when he first shone his torch into Tutankamen's tomb and I wondered if I had been chosen to preserve this marvel for posterity. The feeling persisted into breakfast time and I decided to bow to my fate. It was Sunday morning, but I called a taxi and told the driver to take me to the home of the County Convener. I think he was a Mr Flett, but anyway we were not long at arriving at his farm, and were lucky to get him in the house, having completed his morning's work. He recognised me from the show and immediately got out the bottle. When I told him I had no particular preference of thinner, he said his own choice was Green Ginger which in his opinion developed the bouquet of a wider variety of whiskies than any other additives. I have been a convert ever since. As we sipped the fortified water of life I told him as sincerely as I could of the experience of the day before, and earnestly pleaded with him to open a fund firstly to restore the interior of the shrine to its original glory, then to build a caretaker's house beside it to prevent vandalism, and finally to provide money for its all time maintenance. He seemed enthusiastic so I I gave him £1 to open the account, had a cup of tea brought in by his wife and drove back to Kirkwall where we joined in worship in the famous St Magnus Cathedral with me having at last been freed from the burden that had dominated me for the last twenty hours.

Time is a great forgetter as well as a healer, but you can guess my joy as the fund which I had, I believe, started reached in about four years enough not only repair and restore the chapel, but actually to bring back from Italy to do the work the very man who created it. History will now take over the responsibility of making sure that this simple and lowly shelter is held in fitting reverence by generations yet to come. It is a visible proof of the presence of the living God to whom these simple prisoners of war turned in their hour of hopelessness, and who gave them the ability to demonstrate their faith in His love and protection, by guiding their hands in exquisite artistry as they moulded from debris the symbols of their belief; and clothed them with His presence which prompted — nay, compelled — me to do what I did, in what I consider to be my finest hour.

DOLCE ET DECORUM EST TO KEEP YOUR
COUNTRY THE WAY IT IS

Because we are just a part of the earth which bore and sustained us, we become obsessed with a desire to keep it exactly the way it is, because if it stays as it is, we as an integral part of it must do likewise, and most of us inwardly believe that we are pretty nearly what we would want to be. It follows then that if something occurs which in our view seeks to change in some way society as we have come to accept it, we will do what we can to prevent that change. For centuries, at least fifty to my knowledge, seekers of power have harnessed this human characteristic and used it to further their ambitions either national or global. The technique is to unite their people by persuading them that some threat to their persons or possessions exists and that an all out effort must be mounted to save the fatherland. Whether civilisation has at last discovered the antidote in the form of the atom bomb to the hitherto regular wars and rumours of wars is yet to be found out, but at least it has kept the big boys apart now for thirty-five years.

In the 1930's however, there was no such effective deterrent, so the bully boys could flex their muscles and try to secure for themselves a place in history. The technique was established; you start on the weaklings and work your way up using the subdued (of course you call them liberated) peoples to strengthen your hand.

In the historical period which we are now to discuss, there skulked in Prussia an individual who bore a grudge against the world. He had had the misfortune to be on the losing side in the 1914/18 war, and brooded incessantly about everything, but especially over the fact that some other people seemed more prosperous than he was. To overcome this unacceptable situation, it seemed best to persuade the offenders to leave the district, the nation, or the world. To help towards this end he began to recruit as many co-disgruntleds as he could, howling out of course that everyone else posed a threat to the very life of the Fatherland. Nor was fate satisfied by burdening him with this uncontrollable desire for power and wealth as he had another cross to bear — his name Schickelgruber. There were various alternatives he would have preferred: Captain, Governor, Leader, General, Emperor, President, Deliverer, Messiah; any of these would be an improvement, so things had to be organised towards this end. Persistence brought reward and by 1936 he was well on the way to persuading the other European nations to make up their minds if they wanted to be friendly or non-existent. Here in Britain, which nation had but recently lorded it over three quarters of the earth's population, but which of late had softened because of the affluence which such a situation engenders, we were rejoicing in our new found morality. We had disowned our Schickelgrubers of the past, and there were odd times of the day when the sun was having difficulty in finding a bit of the Empire to shine on. "How good we are," we thought to one another, "that we respect the rights of other people the world over, especially those who have been more bother to keep under control than the value of their gross national product. We have now arrived at the apex of human dignity and anybody that threatens to interfere is going to learn not to the hard way."

I and thousands like me began to be apprehensive about what was going on. With every month that passed, Schickelgruber, now Hitler, was gaining strength. Forever holding marches and rallies, robbing and terrorising groups and individuals, breaking treaties with his neighbours, giving backhanders to amateur athletes and fixing dog races, his actions were international news. To balance matters up and to lull his next victim he would from time to time be seen taking the hand of some small girl and smiling into her eyes with a paternal and caring expression, in the hope that a Reuter correspondent, complete with camera, would forthwith transmit by cable to the world the happy scene with appropriate caption: he loves us all.

It began to be the first thing I looked for in the papers, and I did not like what I read. From a feeling of unease I developed one of unrest, and uncertainty of what I should be doing about it. I pondered with my pals what the consequences to us would be if Western Europe became overrun by a power who had no cause to love us after past encounters. Finally, after much argument with my father, I joined the Territorial Army in the local regiment: the Fife & Forfar Yeomanry. As soon as I signed, a great sense of freedom and relief came over me. I was ready to take on what was coming. This was some time in 1937, and I enthusiastically started my training. It was easy for me I had been working with machinery on the farm, all my life. I had a motor bike of my own, a Rudge Ulster, I could shoot straight, and in a very short time I was promoted twice and held the rank of corporal. I was not however the complete soldier yet, sometimes the polish on my boots did not satisfy our regular army sergeant-major and the angle that my beret sat on my head came in for occasional criticism. Looking me up and down one day in parade he made the following observation, which has come back to me over and over again through forty-three years.

"You're a good bloke, Findlay, and you try hard, but there's one thing I have to say to you, you have no bloody finesse."

He was right though, and it showed on summer camp at Catterick, where the whole regiment was to be inspected by some visiting big shot.

"Get yourself dressed, Corporal," quoth the sergeant-major. "You say you are a shepherd — well go and chase these sheep off the parade ground, and make sure that it is clear for the inspection."

At once I carried out his orders and pursued the woolies to a safe distance, then took up position on the edge of the parade ground to prevent re-entry. As I was strolling back and forward, emitting whistles and the occasional bark, the Colonel and his second-in-command approached, out for their early reconnaisance. I had without thinking re-assumed my civilian calling — I was in charge of things.

"Not a bad kind of a morning, chaps," I said, real friendly like, "I hope it stays fair for the parade."

"I hope so too," returned the Colonel in an off-hand sort of way. "What are you doing here, and don't you see we are in uniform?"

"I am here on the orders of Sergeant-major Willis," I said, "to keep the sheep off the parade ground, and yes, I see you are in uniform."

They moved away leaving me wondering what was biting them. Nor was I long in finding out. I was called in to squadron HQ within the hour, to face a blazing Bill Willis. He fixed me with his glittering eye and let go as only a sergeant-major can. To come face to face with the two most senior officers in the Brigade and fail to salute and to speak without permission — what the hell did I think I was doing, other than disgracing the uniform that I was not fit to wear, and proving myself completely unworthy of the time he had spent trying to make a soldier out of me. He had a bloody good mind to reduce me right down, ignorant bumpkin that I was, and promote someone with more than heather between his ears. Did I have anything to say for myself? I was a soldier now, "No sir," I said, "I will accept whatever punishment you order without complaint."

"That's better, Corporal; you will now check over your troup before the inspection and I hope I never have to have you up again. Dismiss!" From then on I saluted all officers I met regardless of the circumstances or the place.

It would be wrong however for the ambitious OR to carry this practice to the ultimate, as the following true episode will demonstrate.

The training season was interspersed with the usual associated social events such as concerts, sporting contests and regimental dances, where all ranks united in a true spirit of comradeship. One of our toughest NCO's, Corporal Willie Cormie, resplendent in his dress uniform, his scarred and tanned visage flushed with copious beer drinking, was dancing at speed some foxtrot or other. Squadron

CO W.G.N. Walker was also on the floor, but proceeding at a more leisurely pace with the result that the bold corporal was either passing him or crossing his bows. Every time this happened Willie immediately released his right hand from his partner's waist and without losing a beat saluted his CO to which of course the unfortunate Colonel was forced to respond in like. At the conclusion of the dance he approached the group of NCO's of which Willie was one.

"Cormie," he said, "a function like this is not meant to be too formal; it is a sort of friendly get together of everyone in the regiment. On a night like this we can forget that some of us are colonels and others corporals."

Willie stuck out his hand. "Colonel, I like that; from now on I'll be Willie to you and you'll be Willie to me."

Willie some three years later was at it again. This time the regiment was under canvas on the outskirts of Wellingborough, which town held many attractions for socially deprived young men in peak physical condition, and off-duty personnel regularly walked the two miles of an evening to fraternize with the local people, and to help the women folk with the heavier kind of housework which would normally have been undertaken by their husbands at present somewhere else on active service. The CO however took the view that this sort of thing was being overdone and ordered that all ranks had to be in billets by 22.30 hours nightly and that no late passes would be issued. One night SSM Craik, myself, now sergeant, and Willie had been attending a dance where, because of the shortage of men of our age group, we were being generously entertained by the hostesses who by their behaviour demonstrated their delight in our company and the sense of security they felt in our presence. The scene was an exact replica of the activities in Brussels on the eve of Waterloo, when according to the poet hearts were beating happily, but instead of a deep sound interrupting the proceedings about 1 a.m. who should enter the happy gathering but the duty officer, Major J.M. Plain, together with a fellow officer. He expressed considerable surprise to see three of the most senior OR's on a public relations exercise at this time, especially as the CO had warned that he would take an extremely serious view of anyone not in at curfew, but because our previously blameless record, he would drive us home in the back of his van and let the incident pass this time. Grateful for his generosity we piled into the back, and set off. Readers may recall that in wartime all lamps had to be fitted with masks which prevented enemy aircraft from seeing moving vehicles and therefore betraying centres of population. For all the light they gave you you might as well have been using red hot nails, but at least if you were on the same level you could see a vehicle coming towards you.

Such a situation arose in our case, and our driver was in difficulty. He said to his fellow sitting beside him, "I'm damned if I know whether that thing is coming or stationery; his lights do not seem to be moving and he seems to be on our side — I don't know which side of the lights to drive to."

Willie, who had been dozing between Bob and me opened his eyes. "Haud right in atween them sir," he said, and laid back again.

As a warning to others of the dangers of strong drink I may as well relate what was in store for me that same night. Having got past the guard without event — they knew what was good for them — we separated and made for our individual tents, in utter darkness. At the entrance to each tent we had a trench dug, L-shaped and about 9 feet each leg, enough for the eight residents to shelter in during air attacks, but because of recent heavy rains ours had some 3 feet of water in it. Just as I thought I had made it to the tent I fell into it but stayed on my feet and levered myself out. I took about one more step and fell into the other leg, this time hitting my belly on the edge and winding myself. I stood getting my breath back and thinking my luck was not all that good and a feeling of resignation came over me. I folded my arms in front of me, put my head on them and fell asleep up to the waist in water in which position my troop corporal Tom Brunton found me at reveille and pulled me into the tent. I was not one bit the worse for being semi-submerged for over four hours, but it is not a thing I would recommend to my friends.

One more episode in the unorthodox life of the redoubtable lance-sergeant is worthy of putting on record. In the lull before Germany struck us with the blitzkreig a soccer tournament on Brigade lines was held at Montevilliers, and after all but two teams had been beaten, the stage was set for the final. Willie had a lot of money on the team which the rest of us thought had no chance, and many a franc was put up, including a modest 100 of mine, for I had learned by experience that Willie rarely showed all his cards. The reason of his apparent lapse of common sense was revealed to all when the teams took the field. Willie had been appointed referee. He controlled the game with a rod of iron and the favourites could scarcely enter their opponents' half without being ruled offside. Their tackles were penalised, and one of their star players sent off for arguing. In spite of all this Willie's team were unable to score and it looked like ending in a draw. At last however the underdogs floated in a corner kick which bobbed about in front of the goal. Willie was standing in front of the goalie trying to obscure his view when the ball landed on his head which at that moment happened to be rapidly changing direction the better to observe the possibility of any transgression, and the ball landed in the net. Willie immediately signalled a goal and ran to the centre of the field, surrounded by the incensed defenders, one of whom was seen to collapse. He required attention from the side's trainer for a broken nose and slackened molars before the game could be resumed. Because at that time injury time was not added on, the ball was just centred when the referee blew for time, after which Willie collected his vast winnings.

At his court martial he was accused of perverting the natural course of justice, plus assaulting to his injury one centre-half of the 3rd Royal Inniskillin Dragoon Guards. I, as commander of the guard marched him in. His defence was interesting. The goal, he said, was good; if the ball was deflected, no matter whether by friend or foe, the game went on and he had seen more than once in senior football the referee being inadvertently struck when play proceeded. It was a matter of chance that after it had hit him it landed in the net. As for the assault, he had been grasped by his jersey by the tall defender and trying to release himself when the big fellow stumbled. His face accidentally came into contact with the top of the referee's head with the unfortunate result that was the cause of the charge. He was indeed sorry, and wished the unlucky victim a full and speedy recovery. The President of the court was impressed, but having witnessed the whole affair could not bring himself to an acquittal. On charge one, he banned the accused for life from participating in any regimental or brigade competition, on charge two as before, with the exception of boxing as a participant. When I marched him outside and dismissed him Willie appeared deeply offended.

"Jesse," (that was always what he called me after the outlaw Jesse James), he said, "Imagine a — like that getting a commission, do you think I should give him 500 francs for his cut?"

Willie lived through the war and last time I saw him he was playing the piano in a dance band, immaculate in bow tie and dinner jacket, smelling like a florist's shop from a generous application of some body spray the label on which no doubt warned the user of the effects of the contents on women between sixteen and seventy five.

As I will need to cover the events of the overrunning by Germany of the Low Countries and France sometime this seems as good a time as any. As we were in the north we were sent into Belgium to intercept and repel the invaders and got a few kilometres past Brussels before making contact. There was amazing confusion; the roads were jammed with refugees in every kind of transport imaginable from Packards to donkey carts, but mostly on foot, each with a bundle on their back or pushing a loaded barrow, many crying and crippled, dogs, cats, canaries, the lot. They were being incessantly strafed or terrorised by low flying 109's at which we discharged magazine after magazine of 303's from Bren guns and rifles with no visible effect. When aeroplanes are flying at rooftop height it is not easy to get a bead on them; they are out of sight before you can turn if you are in a vehicle as we were (Bren gun carriers). How I longed to get between those poor people and the villains pursuing them but we never did. No sooner had we taken up a defensive position and apparently managed to stop the advance, when within twenty-four hours we would be ordered to retreat to some new line of defence about twenty kilometres in the rear.

Orders were now issued that all males of military age were to be suspected of being German soldiers in disguise who had penetrated our lines to harass the refugees and sabotage bridges and other key communications. It was not at all like what I had imagined and after a few days I began to wonder what was going on. The endless streams of refugees were now being augmented by French and Belgian infantry whose haggard and disorganised appearance did nothing to inspire confidence in anybody, and on every farm the bellows of abandoned cows desperate to be milked was a soul-destroying sound for a man who had worked with stock all his life. Through direct hits and mechanical breakdowns we were losing vehicles daily, but individual units operating over a fairly wide area were ignorant of the overall position and naturally the radio messages from HQ always presented an optimistic picture of the situation. There was one thing we did do; we ate well. There was steak going about in every field, milk likewise, vin blanc and vin rouge in every pub cellar and my own troop had two or three hundredweight of chocolate in boxes from an abandoned factory.

Every now and again orders would come through to hold a certain line, and it always seemed easy. The enemy always broke off and disappeared after about an hour's exchange of fire and we thought "At last," but no, sure enough, sometime through the night would come the order to withdraw, and hold some bridge or village about the usual 15 kilometres to the rear. Soon we were back in France and showing no signs of stopping, and several disturbing new features were appearing. We would meet platoons, or what was left of them, of British infantry which had lost contact with their units and who asked to be taken with us. Not every man was carrying arms and it was about this time I began to doubt if we would ever win the war. The Stukas and Messerschmitts were having the time of their lives. At Caen a whole string of lorries was burned out with about thirty unrecognisable objects in each, which had been men the day before. At Merville a whole line of allied transport planes were machine gunned to hell by wave after wave of 109s. We had our Brens on tripods sitting alongside to defend the transports, but, as I said before, we could not bring them down. My luck was out that day — a single raider came over quite low and not flying very fast and I thought I was sure to get him. I waited till he was almost overhead and pulled the trigger, but alas, the magazine had been badly filled and nothing happened. Before I could replace it he was out of distance having first wounded my next door gunner, Albert Urquhart, in the legs and set the aeroplane nearest us on fire. From a nearby concrete dugout came running an Air Marshal who wanted to know why I had not opened fire. The insult was hard to bear. I looked at the hundreds of empties lying round my gun which I had fired that day while he was somewhere else, but I resisted the temptation and picked up the faulty magazine. "A crossfeed, Sir," I said, "the first I have had in the war." That was the only time I ever met Air Marshal Louis. Strange, I wonder if he remembers the incident.

Anyway, things kept going the same way, until eventually we were told that we were to secure and hold an area of ground round the seaport of Dunkirk from which place we would be reinforced by strong armoured forces whose presence would ensure our ability to master the now over-extended enemy. That evening we retreated through an outer defence line and took up position hull down alongside a road running parallel to the coast, and for once we were thick on the ground. My crew was responsible for a T-junction with a very convenient ditch running alongside the road, into which we each took up position, ante-tank gun, Bren gun, and two rifles. It was a warm evening in June and the hay was ready to be cut. From the house beside the road junction emerged a lady who asked me if I would like coffee, followed by the inevitable "Où sont les allemands?" I accepted the coffee and assured her that les allemands were as near her as they would ever be — she had my word on it.

Alas, next day our outer line withdrew through us and we saw the enemy armour taking occupation of the farm buildings in the distance. We radioed HQ and were rewarded when our artillery shelled the place accurately shortly after. The night was uneventful, but just as daylight was breaking I observed somebody creeping towards me through the hayfield. I was puzzled for he seemed alone, and I could only put his action down to madness or suicide. I lowered the sights of my rifle and waited till I did not think I could miss, not more than 100 yards. From my prone position in the ditch I carefully squeezed the trigger and was satisfied to see the target flatten into the grass. I reloaded and waited for I was sure there must be more when, horror of horrors, my target resumed its crawling approach. Checking my sights I aimed again. At the shot the target jumped up, arms aloft and came running, yelling, "Non, non, cest moi." It was the woman of the house who had gone into the field in darkness to cut grass for her pig and who had been frightened by firing, and was trying to get home. I had missed her both times. The enormity of my crime was too much and I vomited up everything in my stomach. Nevertheless a great realization dawned on me. I knew now there was a God, and he had manifested himself to me that day. I told the lady to stay indoors as long as I was there but if she saw me leaving to come outside and wait until whoever came had searched her house before she went back in. We had started searching houses by first throwing a grenade through the window, and I did not want her inside when the Germans searched it. I never saw her again.

In the forenoon we were visited by our CO, Colonel Sharp, in a carrier to see for himself what was happening. Whatever information he got was not much use to him for he was killed on the road back to HQ, together with a lieutenant badly wounded and Captain Tarcan losing an eye as well as his transport.

About dinner time we got our last order. We were to hold at all costs till 20.00 hours, then retreat towards Dunkirk as far as we could. We should jam up the roads as well as we could with our vehicles, drain the oil from the engines and leave them running full throttle, then proceed to the beach whatever way we could, and we would be taken off by the navy. By late afternoon we were under constant fire and it was not possible for me to get across the road to see how my troop was getting on. I was joined I suppose at about half past seven by about a dozen Welsh Guardsmen who came running along the ditch from my side of the T-road and whose orders were the same. They had held their bit till time was up and were on their way to the beach. They had had it rough, the corporal in charge had only his gas cape on the top half of his body but they all had their arms and were not bowed. They knew that an evacuation was going on, and the corporal it was who made the observation that later was credited to me:

"Our second battalion is standing by to embark to get in behind these bastards, and I'm going with them. Nobody is going to bugger me about like this."

At a few minutes to eight I heard shouting from across the road. It was Corporal Reg Flynn of my squadron who had come back to see what had become of me. He said that we had been told to abandon about an hour ago and it was only when they were moving off he noticed I was not there, and what the hell was I playing at? I told him I was not moving till eight o'clock, to which he replied in that case neither was he and he was coming over the road to join me, which he did forthwith and by the grace of God uninjured. Reg was a big fellow and was dripping with arms of every conceivable kind, even to a Very pistol for sending up flares with. He is a tea planter somewhere about Assam now. He was at that time a tough hot-tempered and reckless chap, whatever he is like now. Many a wrestle we had; he was confident that one day he would back me. (Reg, if you read this, it would not be as difficult now.) At eight o'clock we crawled from the ditch to the back of the house and packed into the Bren carrier, and taking advantage of the cover set out at full speed for Dunkirk.

We came to a point on the outskirts of the town where we could get no further as there were abandoned vehicles blocking everywhere. I knew what my orders were — to drain the oil and run the engine, but I could not force myself to do it. The carrier had been my home and my horse for nearly a year, it had never let me down, though its tarpaulin had a hole through it from a 2lb shell — to murder it was asking too much. I left it ready to start and joined the rest of my little party, but as a gesture of some kind I ran back and switched on the ignition to run down the battery.

It was late evening when we reached the beach, and we did not stop till we were at the water's edge. As luck would have it a rowing boat made straight for us in a matter of minutes and beckoned us to come in and meet it. We waded in till we were up to the chest and were hauled aboard and taken on our way to the mother ship. The sailors wanted us to leave our rifles and everything except our clothing so they could get more people on, but none of us would do it and we landed at Ramsgate next morning armed as we should be and Flynn still looking like a walking arsenal. I think it was a very near thing to us sueing for peace at that time and if freedom is a good thing we have to thank Churchill for it, plus those 21 miles of water that neither tanks, motor bikes nor infantry could cross. From the German point of view this campaign must rank as one of the greatest military feats of all time, in terms of land conquered to time required. I think they were far quicker than they had planned, and were unprepared for our continued resistance. In the light of our experience if the Channel Tunnel goes ahead, I hope we will have a quick way of flooding it should necessity arise.

But back in Ramsgate on that Friday morning with Red Cross, WVS and God knows how many more organisations all wanting to mother and mollycoddle us. I was astonished — we should have been spat on, and their attention reserved for the sailors who really were worthy of the best that could be got. My new-found friends of the Welsh Guards thought they were sure to be sent over again to join their 2nd Battallion somewhere in the south of France, so Reg and I stayed with them hoping to go too. One thing of which I am ashamed was my failure to send word to my parents of my whereabouts, but I had a bad guilt complex until I was able to get back to France somehow and hoped they would never know of our complete rout. For the same reason I refused leave; my father hated losers and I did not look forward to meeting him until I had something better to tell him about.

That summer and autumn of 1940 saw Britain cosmopolitanised in a way not before experienced. Free French, Free Poles, Free Dutch, Free Belgians, Free any damned thing — mostly Colonels and above — at least you never saw a private — and I got my eyes opened by a new facet of human nature: the instinct of survival. Although the behaviour of the French and Belgian women was liberal in the extreme, somehow I had expected this, partly from the stories of the 1914/18 boys and partly because I believed that for any other nationality of female, a Scottish soldier was bound to be the right person to be dating. The shock of seeing British women practically lying down in front of any foreigner they could get near enough to was severe enough to cause me to rethink values.

Out of my sergeant's pay of forty-two shillings I had been banking £1.6 shillings weekly because my needs were nil, or nearly nil, and by selling my tobacco allowance the £1 or so a week I was left with had been ample. I now adopted SM Jock Stewart's motto: "What is there to worry about? We will all be dead in a year anyway", and anybody who saw Coventry or Swansea the day after their bombing would have had to admit there was some chance. Soon I was behaving in the newly accepted morality in a way which can best be described as a cross between that of an Inverbraw grousebeater and a butcher's dog, and instead of saving money I was withdrawing it.

In January 1941 I came home on leave. I came off the bus at Dundee (the sight once more of which city from the train coming over the Tay Bridge had brought tears to my eyes) and there was my father waiting for me at the road end. He was but a shadow of the man I had parted from eighteen months before and I hardly recognised him.

"By God, Dad," I said, "You are working too hard, how is mother?" "She is away at Mrs Grant's funeral," he said, "Mine will be in a week or two."

He was wrong. It was almost three months, and he was as much a casualty of the war as any soldier. He had been a pioneer in hill land management and as far back as 1929 had established a herd of cross Highland cows at Hatton Hill and treacherous brutes they were. As stockmen will know, some of them hide their calves and only return to suckle them for about the first four days, and woe betide anything, specially dogs or humans, that either consciously or inadvertently gets too near the calf. As we did not know any better at that time we accepted this sort of behaviour as an occupational hazard, and I had developed a strategy to deal with it. As Hatton Hill was not drained at that time, there were innumerable boggy bits, and I simply ran into one of them pursued by the angry cow. This was where she made a mistake, for no sooner had I got her in the marches with her mobility reduced, than I turned on her, seized her by the head, twisted her neck and couped her. Then I would lay into her till she was exhausted and I could make good my escape. Although my father disapproved of what I did, he did not forbid it (in fact years later I learned he had offered to wager George McIntosh of Cormuir that I would coup any Cormuir cow that attacked me and if he would send some of his worst ones down to the Hatton, he would get them back a lot civiler next time they calved), but he maintained you should never run from an animal, and that they would avoid hitting you at the last moment. As I knew he would go to the hill alone when I was away, this was one of the things I entreated him to be careful about for I knew the last thing in a charging cow's mind was to avoid the object of its wrath. I also knew that no matter what I said he would do it his way, but at least I tried. In the event I was proved correct, he was knocked over and kneed not long after I was mobilized. His broken ribs healed again but some irreparable damage was done to his chest and throat which developed into the cancer which killed him. The grieve, Duncan Pirie, who had brought him down from the hill, and whose arrival on the scene had prevented the cow killing him on the spot, identified the attacker. She was henceforth named Alex Findlay and was a danger to everybody for rest of her life.

Knowing what I know now, it should be made a serious criminal offence for anybody to keep an animal known to be dangerous. The Israelites of Biblical times were right on the ball. Exodus XI verse 28 states "If an ox gore a man or a woman, that they die then the ox shall be surely stoned and his flesh shall not be eaten but the owner of the ox shall be quit, but if the ox were wont to push with his horn in time past and it hath been testified to his owner, and he hath not kept him in, but that he hath killed a man or woman, the ox shall be stoned and his owner also shall be put to death." What an example of what a law should be, clearly defined and easily understood. The benefit to society of such a law is apparent in the universal docility of the bovine species of the Middle East.

The state of my father's health was evidently known to the authorities because my unit ordered me to take extended leave to a date not yet fixed, but to report to the Home Guard and take orders in the meantime where I could use my qualifications gained from courses at Hythe and Bovington. (I instructed on small arms and hand to hand combat as well as the usual discipline forming exercises, like marching and boot polishing.) My father, after an unsuccessful operation, died on 21 April, after three months of misery borne with his usual fortitude. A day or two before the end he said to me, "I'm dying, Jim, but I don't care, I've done most of the things

I wanted to and I want you to have more interests than just work, take a shooting maybe, or do the trials, we all have a good way with dogs.''

Shortly after his burial I got another letter from the War Office. I was transferred to Class W Reserve and seconded to the Angus Battallion, Home Guard, with the rank of lieutenant and was required to report to my old unit to pick up my personal belongings and documentation. It was a savage blow, for we had learned a lot, and there were some Germans I wanted to resume acquaintance with in case they had got the wrong impression that last time; but the authorities were adamant that I was better employed in the national interest at home. With a heavy heart I look my leave from my squadron at Wellingborough, complete with a certificate from our new CO, Colonel Mullens, that my conduct during the time on active service had been exemplary. I suppose most people get a thing like that to help to dull the pain of getting transferred from a regiment that has become their life.

I suppose that for the next three years or so I was the most unpopular person in Angus. The new training technique Battle Innoculation had arrived, and I forced numerous well-meaning but ignorant volunteers to endure conditions as near to the real thing as I could, without actually killing anybody. Some of the disillusioned or terrified members adopted whatever means open to them to escape, like staying off work next day on medical grounds, thereby ensuring that their employer would complain to the CO and get them excused parade. I was actually asked by the CO, Major Methven, to ease off as I was treating volunteers like conscripts, and subjecting them to greater physical effort than they could reasonably be expected to endure. I thought of the people of France and Belgium, from infants in arms to great-grandmothers, trudging along the dusty roads, till they would walk no further, gunned and bombed without respite, and thanked the Lord once more for the English Channel, which alone had prevented like conditions here, and I was determined that any force for which I was responsible would not be panicked no matter what happened. It came to a head when one night I sent a party to bring an absentee in front of me, and gave them half an hour. He appeared in slippers and night-shirt well within the time, feeling very ill-used, and prophesying that I would hear more about this, his employer being on very good terms with the CO. I was again warned that I was overdoing things, and told that on no account was I again to pull people who had been working all day out of bed. Thank goodness, by this time we were beginning to get the upper hand, and Cologne, Dusseldorf and Berlin were getting repaid for Coventry, Swansea and London, so I could afford to ease off, with a clear conscience.

After victory when we were all paraded in the Market Muir at For-far, the Earl of Airlie addressed the assorted and motley mob. He was an exceptional figure of a man with a distinguished career both in peace and in war. (I later got to know him well in the County Council).

"The nation thanks you all," he said "for guaranteeing the safe-ty of our beloved motherland, for well I know what you would have done had the enemy been foolhardy enough to invade us."

For a horrible moment I thought he was to tell us, but his natural good manners saved the situation. For those of us who participated and survived, 1939-45 was an experience that can never be forgot-ten, exposing as it did the extremes of human dignity and degrada-tion from the heroes of Arnhem and Dieppe to the ghouls of Belsen and Auschwitz. Whether wars on this scale are of eventual benefit or disadvantage to humanity is open to argument, so I will close this episode with the story of the stockbreeder who had been expelled from his society for faking pedigrees and had to hand over to his son: "Well Bertie, the herd is yours now, and you can manage it whatever way you like, the honest or the crooked way — I've tried them both and there's hellish little in it."

THE ELEMENT OF CHANCE

In 1950 there was produced a document called *The Tay Valley Plan*. The rebuilding of the war-damaged cities was progressing apace and the new concept of National Planning was the 'in thing' so that natural and national assets should be preserved and added to, while virgin areas were to be developed in a way which would enhance their appearance, and would provide either work or recreation for the community.

So, when it came to Strathmore's turn to be planned, and the pro-posals for the future were published, and the plans displayed in public places, those of us affected were naturally interested to see what was in store.

Imagine my horror therefore to discover that the field in front of my house was earmarked as a public playing field, complete with chutes, swings, jungle area and paddling pool. The Castle Park — that is its name because of Hatton Castle being in it — was the field where the milk cows grazed, where the tups lived before the sales when they had to be brought inside at a moment's notice to keep them dry, and where my father practised his dogs for the trials, and the proposal to change it as outlined above seemed to me to be worse than all the other sins I could think of put together. I could hardly wait till night to get down to the Councillor, Brigadier W.R. Mac-donald of Kirkton House. I had known him since childhood; he travelled to Dundee daily in a chauffeur driven Wolseley to his office at St Roque's Garage where he and another brigadier, Frank Hibbert, ran this high class garage. W.R. never quite forgot his army rank, and as I was being ushered into his presence by his charming wife I thought with some satisfaction: "This is one time when I'm in front of a red tabs, and there's nothing he can do about it."

After the usual pleasantries he asked me the purpose of my visit, as his wife had indicated that I had said it was urgent when I phoned. I told him what I had seen in the Post Office window and had confirmed from the press about my field, and expressed my acute disappointment that he, whom I trusted to look after my interests, had allowed such a thing to happen. I continued something like:

"Brig, I really admire you as a soldier, there are hundreds of useless lieutenants, and a good few captains as well, but from major up they are pretty good men and anybody getting the length you have got to has to be admired and respected. I would like to think as much of you as a councillor as I do as a soldier, so here's what I want you to do. Go to whoever is responsible for designating my field for anything else than it is and get him to leave it alone, and publish the fact so there is no misunderstanding. Have it done in two months, and I will say you are a really good councillor. If you don't I'll oppose you at the next election and beat you as hard as I can."

He looked at me for a long time and I wondered if he was to shout "Guard!", but when he spoke it was controlled, even friendly.

"You know, Jim, I haven't been feeling all that well recently and I have been wondering who to try to get to take over. The last ten minutes has solved my problem. I'll resign tomorrow, and bring out nomination papers. I'll be one of your proposers and help in the election. You'll win all right and you can sort out the field yourself."

So, there I was neatly trapped, outmanoeuvred by a master tactician, with nothing for it but to start the canvassing. I was opposed by a young man who was doing well demolishing over-large mansions, castles, churches etc., and selling the reuseable items like oak staircases, mural ceilings, ornamental railings and the like, to the "nouveaux riches" who wanted to incorporate a bit of the past into their new villa or four-apartment house.

He was an ambitious young man, and would have done well in local government, but the nostalgia of the war was still strong, anybody who had been at Dunkirk was popular, and though I had ill-used a lot of the men by tough training in the Home Guard, I seemed to have been forgiven and I won convincingly.

Thus I launched into a job that I have held ever since. My electors continue to return me with an enthusiasm that obliges me to give it all I have got to try to be worthy of the trust of such fine people.

The amendment of the plan regarding the field at Newtyle duly materialised. I am glad I did what I did, because Hatton Castle is now to be restored to its former glory and I unwittingly saved its policy park. One day in 1960 Sir James said to me "Could you come up to Alrick on Saturday morning? I would like you to meet my son Jim, the banker, and to have a look round the place with us." I accepted at once; he was so nice, I could do no other, so up I went, to be introduced to J.G.S., all 6'4" of him, eyes that looked through you as well as at you, lean and tanned, and I thought "some boy this". I learned that he was amongst other things a Chartered Accountant, a Director of the Clydesdale Bank, that he had five sons and a daughter and a love of Scotland. We motored and walked round the estate in the afternoon, discussing shelterbelts, reseeding, deer control, Blackface sheep, cross Hereford cows, cross fences, number of men needed, farm buildings, everything you could think of. Just before I left for home after tea, when Sir James was seeing me to my car he said "Now that you have seen over the place, and heard what we would like to do, if the place was yours do you think you could make it pay?"

The alarm bells in my brain started clanging, and I thought hard for something acceptable to say.

"Well, Sir James, what with the various grants going just now, I think I could make the place better without losing money anyway, so I suppose you could say it was paying."

"Well J.F. (that's what he always called me until his last year when he changed to Jim) it's been great having you up. I'll see you at the Council on Monday." Sure enough, after Council business he took me to one side. "J.F." he said, "after you left on Saturday, Jim and I had a long talk. We want you to handle Forter the way we spoke about. We are not to sell it to you but we have decided to make you and Jim partners. He will provide the capital and you the knowhow. I'll do the office work and help if I may?"

As I have said you did not say no to Sir James. but I said I would make the final decision after a further meeting with Jim. The meeting took place in my house on the Saturday next. It took about ten minutes, and the bargain struck was, that I was ₁o run the estate on a plan agreed between us, and always to keep his father informed and consulted because it would make him so happy to see the glen going again. For his part he would manage my affairs to the best financial advantage.

So that was it — I had to make Sir James happy and Jim had to make me rich. I think 24 years on we can both say we carried out our promises.

In the years of partnership which lasted until our respective sons people.

The amendment of the plan regarding the field at Newtyle duly materialised. I am glad I did what I did, because Hatton Castle is now to be restored to its former glory and I unwittingly saved its policy park.

A few years after I joined the Council, I think about 1955, a new man was elected to represent Glenisla, another ex army officer, Gen. Sir James Gammell, from Alrick, and I formed a great respect for him. Although nearly all the convenerships were held by landed gentry at that time it seemed the natural thing, and we trusted them to be doing the right thing without too much participation from us back benchers.

Somehow I got on particularly well with two of the big boys, The Earl of Airlie and Sir James. The Earl, as Lord Lieut. of Angus did not hold a convenership and he sat next me in Committee, and our mutual interests in agriculture gave us a common topic of conversation. I was having it good with the sheep about this time and he used to mention it occasionally. He never called me anything but Findlay, yet I never resented it I don't know why. With General Gammell however I formed a deeper relationship he was one of the two best mannered men I ever knew (Roy Waterston of Crichton Mains was the other) he was developing his recently acquired estate of Forter and was intensely interested in what I was doing on Hatton Hill. In due course Nan and I were invited up to Alrick and regular family visits developed both ways.

One/day in 1960

were farming on their own account, and fit to take over their respective estates, I never had a wrong word with Sir James. He was a fitness fanatic and could walk me into the ground on Mount Blair or Car Nan Feidhen, and he was about the only human being that my big dog Roy passed the time of day with. When he finally succumbed I was glad that I had been up to see him two days previously — he had said in his usual bright way: "Jim, I fear this hill is a bit too much for this old horse to get over. I think my M has something for you to remind you of our friendship."

After the funeral Lady Gammell gave me his gold cufflinks. Marcus will get them in due course, and I hope he appreciates them, for if Jim has made me rich in money, my association with his father was for me a pearl without price.

As well as with Sir James, I had a very happy relationship with two of the families who worked on Forter. We employed five regular men, their wives when we could and their children at weekends, as well as students and casuals, fencers and dykers etc. Naturally I was closest to the ones that I employed, those who were there before me could not be expected to take kindly to new management but I was as gentle as I could be with them because it was their way of life that was being interfered with.

We all respected Joe Robertson, the estate keeper. Nobody knew how old he was, certainly he was the chap who the runners of the hill race had to go round at the top as long as the oldest inhabitants could remember. My father won that race sometime in the 90's, but Joe could not remember this when I asked. By my time he just worked when he liked but he liked it often and most of the shelterbelts were planted by him. He had deep green fingers, as the saying goes. Every tree he planted was cocking its lugs within a week, and if we managed to keep the deer off they were trees in no time. If Wren wanted to be known by the buildings that lived after him, anyone travelling the Forter Dalnaglar road that links Glenisla and Glenshee is a witness to the contribution Joe Robertson made to the glory of wooded hills.

The Grieve at Forter until he died was John Kinmond, ably and energetically assisted by his wife Mary, and his grandchildren in the summer holidays. John was a good and conscientious man, possibly better at arable work than handling livestock, but that is where Mary excelled. There was latterly 75 cows and their calves at his steading, and Mary was in her element amongst them. Hardly a cow but she could approach on the hill, some of them followed her to the gate when she was leaving them. I would say that next to Andrew Lindsay of Tipperty, mentioned elsewhere, she was gifted with cattle. John lost his fight with leukaemia while still at his best, and Scotland was the poorer for his passing. Mary lives in Alyth now; I go to see her once in a while and we have a blether about the old times.

The family I got to know best were the Aitkens; Jock and his German wife Inge, their two sons Nicholas and Ronald and their daughter Elizabeth. Inge always fed me at handlings or when we were dykeing or draining, and Jock was a real good hill shepherd. I feed him from a flat farm in Strathmore and of course Sir James appeared on his first morning to take him round the hill, setting out as Jock said "like a greyhound out of a trap". Before dinner time he had Jock absolutely exhausted, although that is not the word Jock used when he told me. The two of them always got on well, and eventually Sir James called him Jock instead of Aitken, the only one of our workers so honoured.

They did not get off to the best of starts either; Sir James broke a golden rule by visiting the new man before they had all the flitting into place in the house and wellmeaningly welcomed the harassed couple and hoped they would enjoy living in such an attractive house quite recently modernised. "Maybe it's modernised," said Jock, "but it's filthier than a bloody pigs crae and, if ever there was blind rollers, there's none now — come back after we get it cleaned." Sir James never mentioned the incident to me; it was Jock who told me some years later. When Jock got settled in we started to rebuild the slaps in the March dykes round the hill and I marvelled at the way they were built, with the smaller stones at the bottom and great brutes of up to 2 cwts at the top. Though it was tempting to get rid of the big ones low down, the finished job always looked a patch, so we decided the big ones were to go back where they belonged. Sometimes it was as much as the two of us could do to get them up and I used to think the original dykers must have been supermen, but we never gave in. Some years later I was down at Meigle having a crack with Andrew Scrymgeour, at that time nearly 80, who had spent his working life of some 70 years contracting draining, fencing, dykeing, and tree planting all over Scotland and who had made his firm, A. Shepherd & Co, Meigle, famous for industry and integrity. Local authorities accepted without question his tenders, even if he was the sole offerer. He told me that when he erected the fence along the rigging of Mount Blair most of the iron posts had to be leaded into holes jumpered into the rock and the squad lived in a tent on the hill for a week at a time, replenishing their food store on Sunday night with provisions procured by their women folk on the Saturday. I said to him that night: "They must have been some men who built the Dalnaglar dyke, Andrew; some of the big stones I could hardly lift to the top."

"Surely you did not try to lift up the cops," said Andrew. "We gaed ower that dyke about 45 years ago; the big stones have to be on the top so deer and sheep cannot dislodge them, but you dinna lift them — you rowe them up a plank.''

It is so simple when you know how! I must have forgotten about the Pharoahs using this device in the form of ramps to get the pyramids built. Andrew and his men with their planks were 20th century Remeses.

One of the jobs we did in Glenisla and which has, I think, a good chance of lasting for ever, was when we straightened the Isla at Muckle Doonies. The huge loop, properly called an oxbow, had been over the centuries responsible for the loss of many a field of stooks by holding back storm water, flooding the haughs and taking crops with it as it subsided. Jim G. got agreement with Harry Gibb, who owned the other side, for us to dig a new river bed with no obstruction which, as well as saving flood loss, would enable us both efficiently to drain our respective riverside fields. The feeling I had when the bulldozers cut the last few yards and the river surged gloriously into its new home, was one of triumph mixed with just a little bit of doubt that anybody really had the right to do things of this kind. If somebody ever does a little engineering job and lets the salmon and sea trout up the Isla it would considerably enhance the sporting attraction and the economy of one of our most beautiful glens.

Here is a little story about one dinnertime in the Aitken house at a speaning when Inge was feeding some five incomers with her usual enthusiasm. It was the 13th of August and the postie came with the Courier just as we were at our dinner — where we come from, dinner is at midday and supper is in the evening. The great interest, of course, on this date, to hill men, is how the "Glorious Twelfth" has turned out and how the various beats had done this year (last year's figure in brackets) and Jock read out aloud so we could all be informed at once. "Glenmoy 46 brace 6 guns, Gamochy 102 brace 10 guns, birds plentiful but wild, Lednathie 7 guns had 32½ brace and 11 various, Remony, Mr Duncan Millar and four of a party shot 26 brace walking; again birds were strong and wild.''

"Hold on, Jock," I said, "there's something wrong there; the grouse couldn't have been very wild if they managed to shoot them walking.''

Jock fell in right up to the lugs. "For God's sake Jim," he said, it was the fowk that were walking, nae the grouse.''

Jock stayed on at Forter when Jamie, Jim's eldest son took over from me. He and Inge now live in Newtyle and both work at Liff Hospital, but Jock always takes his holidays at the Blackface shows and sales. He sometimes sends me a book by Lillian Beckwith or James Herriot. His family have all done well and, in common with the Kinmonds, they left Glenisla in better shape than they found it. I value their friendship a lot.

Before I start on Lundie and Aucharroch I must relate a story that stays on in my mind. My grieve at Hatton for some years was one Bob Lumsden, who came to me as a tractorman and took over as grieve when the foreman thrashed the man who held the job after some quarrel in a potato field and he could not bear the shame of it and left. Bob's biggest asset was his wife Margaret, a fine woman in every sense of the word who, having brought up her family, worked out at the harvest and the potato dressing, an operation which needed 10 people. This December afternoon — and a beautiful one it was — we were ready for a shift up the pit and the engine of the dresser was stopped till we got reset. Bob, always a great cracker, was elucidating on the events of the day, prominent amongst which was the headline in the paper that some film actress or other had just married her third husband. Bob had strong views about this sort of behaviour and hastened to put us in the picture.

"There's nae need to carry on like that; that's what I would ca' legalised whoring; beasts dinna behave like that. One woman should be plenty for any man and I should ken, for look at her and me" (indicating with his index finger his spouse busily engaged tidying up round the machine). "We have gaen thegither since we were at the school and never looked at any other body since." He paused to reflect, then continued: "Do you ken, when we started to go thegither we were really young — so young we didn't know what to do."

Bob's startled better half interrupted: "Will you hold your tongue."

Bob, however, was too far committed to stop. "But we helped one anither and in nae time we were getting on like a house on fire." I was down celebrating with them their 70th marriage anniversary last year and they are still happily helping each other as they did in 1900 when they attended Glamis school together. Two of their three sons gave their lives for the rest of us in the war. Alex, their youngest, stays with them and is repaying their love and care in time gone by.

As I said earlier, I often cried in on Andrew Scrymgeour for a blether, or rather I stayed to chat after I had told him to erect some new fence or other, and how I wish I could have taped some of his boundless store of country lore. He knew exactly how many yards of a 6 wire fence a squad (usually 4) should put up in a day, likewise dykeing and draining. Queer how dyke has two opposite meanings! In the fens of England it is a water course or ditch; with us it is a lot of stones built dry some 4' high and 2' at the base to form a division between fields or to form roadside boundaries. Sometimes the art is referred to by those who do not know any better as "dry-stone dykeing" but, seeing there is no other kind in Scotland at least, the dry-stone bit is quite superfluous, and jars on my nerves not quite so much as "never ever" which sends a shiver right down to my toes but about the same as "in point of fact" or "at this moment in time".

This night in June 1966, Andrew said "I had a phone call from David Simpson this morning needing some fences sorted pretty urgently because he has decided to sell Aucharroch. Aucharroch! I was born on the Barnton, that's the other farm on Aucharroch. It is one of the best livestock farms in the district, the calves and lambs are always among the best at the backend sales, it would be a right farm for you."

I had always wanted a farm of my own! I had asked once or twice if Sir James Cayzer would sell me the Hatton, but he would not, so I phoned my partner, Jim Gammell, who told me to find out the price and go over the farm and let him know.

I made an appointment for the next day and was taken round by David, who was delighted that I was interested. When we were having tea he said, "When we decided to sell I said to Betty wouldn't it be grand if Jim Findlay bought it — he's pretty well finished at Hatton, and he would be the very man to make a job of Aucharroch." I asked what the price was, lock, stock and barrel, and he said he had a valuer over it who estimated £100,000 but if I would let him shoot and fish any time he wanted and give him a beech tree occasionally for firewood he would take £80,000. I went home and phoned Jim; he came up next day and we looked it together.

"He is not asking too much," was Jim's verdict, "You buy it for your own, but if you want we will farm it under the partnership and we will really be equal, me with Forter and you with this. You will need to borrow a bit to pay this amount without selling something you should be keeping, so if you have any bother with your own bank the Clydesdale will be pleased to accommodate you."

I went up to Aucharroch next day to clinch the deal, I tried David with £78,000 but when the hurt expression came on his face I said I was joking, he would get his £80,000. "Well Betty, that's business settled," quoth David, "Would you make a cup of tea?" The whole thing had not lasted five minutes and I was now the owner of 722 acres, two farmhouses, three cottar houses, a mile of half of the Quharity river, and an overdraft of £30,000. To be owing anybody such a sum kept dinning into my head all the way home, I had become used to being in the black and that night I would have given a lot to cancel the whole thing. The mood persisted next day while we were gathering Mount Blair for dipping and I had a strong urge to slip over the edge of the rocks and honourably end it all. The thought of Nan and the children prevailed and prevented too serious contemplation of the easy way out, and the depression gradually lessened until in about a week I was used to the idea of a debt burden and beginning to enjoy being a laird.

To get a picture of what fate had allocated to me we have to go back a couple of years. The factors for Newtyle Estate were J. & H. Pattullo, Donald, Dundee and the senior partner by this time was Roy Matthewson for whom we had formed a high opinion because of his fair dealings and straight talking. I had got him to represent me in any matter needing legal training and we visited each other quite frequently. If our tenant.factor relationship had been the norm, Burns would have had to re-write The Twa Dogs. In retrospect maybe Roy was too much a tenant's man, but he knew that a million or two was not going to make much difference to the Laird, so I think we tenants on Newtyle were not too badly done by (notice I use the past tense).

I got a message one day asking me to phone, to be told by Roy "You know we look after the late Charles Walker's estate at Lundie, beside Edzell. We had a meeting with Harry, and he wants you to manage it for him, as he wants to stay in the army for a while yet."

Harry had been my troop officer in the war; he had not been put on Class W in the middle of it but had won the MC and by this time was a Brigadier. Although of commissioned rank, when he joined us he was just an overgrown boy and I kind of felt responsible for him, for it was obvious that if he survived he would be a lot of use.

My initial reaction was to agree, but then I wondered what the last twenty years had done to him, and I also wondered what Jim Gammell would think if his partner undertook extra commitments so I phoned him for a start. It lets you see the man Jim is, for he encouraged me to take on the job; both our sons were growing up and they would soon need some responsibility, he said, so I arranged a meeting with Harry. He was just the same as always, bubbling with self assurance, he had married a very beautiful Danish countess, had four children and the world was at his feet. He was now an authority on armoured warfare, and was in the way of demonstrating our Churchill tanks to other NATO countries with a view to getting them to buy them.

The two of us picked up where we had left off in 1941, but this time the roles were reversed, I gave the orders and he paid the men.

The bargain I made with him was that for £1,000 a year I would develop his estate into a productive agricultural unit if he would stick in and become the youngest Field Marshal in the British Army. I had heard that there was an outstanding grieve on the place and I wanted to get into his good books right away, so as soon as I made the bargain with Harry, I told him I was going down to meet the grieve.

"That's a good idea," said Harry, "Nicol is a fine chap, he was born on the place, his father was grieve before him, and Mrs Nicol is really good as well."

"Right, I'll just go and meet him now, but I'll need to know his name," I said,

"Nicol is his name, it would be if his wife is Mrs Nicol, surely," answered the puzzled Brig.

"Man, Harry, I know that," I said, "It's his first name I want, what is it?"

After a long pause, Harry said, "Damn it, I don't know, I think it's possibly John."

Before I went down to the farm I asked the clerkess, and all my life since when I think of or have a crack with Will Nicol, I know that he fills to a T the description of Arthur Street's hero in *The Gentleman of the Party*.

Of all the estates I have set foot on, Lundie has the most. Whether you want to grow strawberries, marigolds, oats, barley mushrooms or rhododendrons, it will respond with a will. With its grouse moor, pheasant shoot, abundance of ground game and its three lochs at different altitudes, there just is not a rural pursuit that is not catered for, and I was determined to safeguard one and all. Eleven hundred and fifty-four acres all told, nearly all south lying, admirably protected from destructive winds by natural topography or well planted woodlands, eligible on the higher land for the various production grants and livestock subsidies, it was as near independent of the need to purchase anything but diesel oil, as could be dreamed of.

Some time in the misty past a bullock had fallen over the rocks at the bit known as Parklands, a 202 acre practically flat plateau bounded by the west Water River provided by a genial providence in case some laird of Lundie liked salmon fishing, and Harry's father had put this bit out of bounds as far as livestock was concerned. I had read that in British Columbia there are miles and miles and hundreds of miles of deep black loam so far undisturbed by man and I had a feeling that I had discovered a wee bit that had got lost. The first thing I did was to get on the telephone to Andrew Scrymgeour and tell him to fence the complete march and take in every ploughable yard, while rendering it safe for all classes of livestock. Then I got Jim Fearn who had ploughed chunks of Forter for me to put three tractors with prairie buster type ploughs to blacken it. It was so big and irregular in shape we ploughed it round and away from the centre and Will Powrie told me the only time a tractor stopped ploughing was when the driver had to pass water. I do not think we had a bogey load of stones off the whole field, a thing that puzzled me until I realised that sometime in the distant past the Picts or Druids, or when you think of it, probably the Stone Age Men, had used them all to construct the nearby White Catherun fort with its outer and inner protective stone ramparts, built from stones passed from man to man along a human chain which must have reached a mile or more.

606 tons of lime on the ploughing, 3 turns of the discs, 50 tons of 24.11.11, 37 lbs per acre of my favourite SAI grass seed mixture, and we had a new farm capable of carrying 80 cows and 120 ewes. We bought 150 cross Hereford Irish bred heifers at Mirklands docks: I took William Nicol with me to get him used to Irish cattle dealers who confused the value of their beasts with the national debt. Prices were relatively stable in the Sixties and my price for a bulling heifer that looked like being a kind mother was £57. With my own needs, plus getting some for other people, I must have bought over one thousand in that decade.

To keep them comfortable in the winter we built two new courts for 150 each, which made all the farms I was responsible for alike with units in multiples of 75. I only used one bull, the Lincoln, at Aucharroch, other than Aberdeen Angus; my loyalty to Hugh Watson, whose grave in Newtyle Churchyard I and Bob Adam got the Society to restore, was complete, but I always selected a rangier type bull than the Argentinians. I suppose amongst my better accomplishments was managing to win first prize for the best pen of eight homebred yearling bullocks at the great spring show and sale held by McDonald Fraser of Perth eight years in succession. The first year that they made over £100 each, I stopped at Burrelton on the road home and bought a carton of ice cream for Nan and the children.

But back to Lundie — in three years Will Nicol and I had it beginning to fizz; we had got a useful shepherd and purebred the best ewes to become self sufficient in their sheep — we even sold a few tup lambs quite successfully. Then word came that Harry had suffered a heart attack, while demonstrating tanks to Leopold of the Belgians, and was to retire from the Army. Sure enough, in a few months the family took up permanent residence in the Castle, with Harry looking as fit as ever and also as fully of the joys.

The saying about the cooks and the broth seemed to me to be about to be demonstrated if I continued as if nothing had happened, so I told Harry that I proposed to discontinue my role and my salary, but to make myself available as a friend whenever needed. I thought it was the right thing to do at the time, and was not to forsee the tragedy that was to follow. The doctors had told Harry not to take excessive exercise, probably not excessive drink either, though I do not know that, but Harry told me he was to ignore them and not to be dictated to by anybody who had not heard about Thomas Mordaunt: "One crowded hour of glorious life is worth an age without a name." Suiting his actions to his words he had gone up Lethnot one September day to attend a grouse shoot and his splendid labrador bitch had collapsed and died. He had brought her home in the Land Rover, had his tea and a wash up then gone to bury her in a corner of the ground, where in a short time he was found dead beside the grave he had newly dug.

Fate played it rough with Harry Walker, he would have gone to the top in the Army but for its interference and I was encouraging him all I could to distinguish himself as a land owner and agriculturalist. He had shortly before his death purchased the nearby farm of Reidhall, very much against my advice, and when I got the news of his death I prepared to take over for the sake of Patsy and their children, so I phoned Roy Matthewson to find out if he had left any instructions, only to be told by Roy that Harry had transferred his business to an Arbroath firm of lawyers. I went to see Patsy to be told that the new executors had appointed Gordon Porter of Scryne to advise and manage the estate until things were tidied up. I have often worked with Gordon on matters agricultural and I like him a lot. He phoned apologising for what had happened and offered to stand down but I insisted that he should go on according to the family wishes. The next I heard was that three sets of death duties in seven years was forcing Lundie on to the market while Patsy was to continue farming in Reidhall and that is exactly what happened. The gentleman of the party, true as ever to his trust, stayed on with the new owners, a family of Macdonalds who were expanding at a rate of knots at the time, but for reasons of which I am unaware they resold in about five years time at a profit of several hundred thousand pounds. The new owner, one Patrick Thomson, lasted no longer than his predecessors, and this magnificent unit has now been sold off in seven or eight different lots, and is now in the way of worsening the barley surplus. There is not an animal to be seen, and very seldom a human. This time reality has taken over from A.G. Street's fiction and the gentleman has moved to manage another estate where I hope and confidently expect his new employers appreciate his worth. There's a good bit of Homeriggs Ben in Will Nicol; he never seemed to be in a hurry, but he was always in the right place at the right time. I will conclude the story of my dealings on or with estates by relating the events which decided me to sell Aucharroch.

In 1966 when I bought it I started on a four year plan to make it the farm that people would speak about. I employed two drainage contractors and gave them a side apiece. David Winter got the job of rebuilding every dyke and cementing the copestones, Reekie Engineering rebuilt the two steadings, we planted shelter blocks, tarmaced the road, modernised the farmhouse and cottages, and employed five men and their womenfolk to look after the crops and animals, and tried to put it right for my son when he would be ready to take over. This time fate had a go at me for Marcus married at a very young age one Stella Spence whose father owned the estate of Biel in East Lothian, and who with commendable generosity presented the pair with the magnificent farm of Pitcox as a wedding gift. As Jamie Gammell was at an age when he too was ready for a position of authority, I decided to come out of the Gammell & Findlay partnership, give up the lease of Hatton, where I had spent the last forty-two years, and concentrate all my energies on Aucharroch and local government, for about this time I was appointed Vice-Convener of the County. I had been chairman of the Magistrates for a year or two and these commitments were demanding an increased share of my time. I was lucky of course to have Joe Troup who will be famous one hundred years from now, and Hamish McKay is a good hand at bringing out sheep. The culmination of all these factors came in 1972 when we won the Best Farm in Angus Competition, was reserve for the Best Farm in the North-East of Scotland, and topped all the sales of both Blackface and Border Leicesters we sold. Counting children there were 27 people living on Aucharroch that year.

I suppose my very success had something to do with ensuring events because my employees became the target for ambitious employers and first Hamish and then Joe got posts with greater responsibility and prospects than they had with me. Though Harold Habblett — I had engaged his father out of the commandoes for foreman at Hatton, where as aforetold he cost me one grieve — took over quite satisfactorily from Hamish, I had a very poor response when I advertised Joe's job, and made a very unhappy choice of a replacement who I was glad to see depart in a very short time, so I decided to get a novice and train him. The young man I took meant well, but I realised I was no longer fit for the heavy end of things, my back was now suspect since my bronco-busting episode, and both my knees became exceedingly painful walking rough ground, to the extent that I was often late at a gate when shedding or moving animals. I consulted doctors and the like, some thought it was cartilage trouble and would need an operation, some said rest.

The wheel had turned full circle in four years; I was now struggling to keep one farm going where previously five had been easy. Marcus was settled at Pitcox, Jane was getting married to an architect, and Sally was still at primary school. It all happened quite suddenly. Ian and Jennifer Thomson and their two girls visited us annually about early June for a walk round the farm to see the new crop of lambs and calves. By chance that night Colin McLean of Keillor turned up and accompanied us round the farm. My knees were giving me pure hell but there was one Blackface tup lamb I wanted them to see, and as we were unable to get him on the hill I knew that

The people who worked and lived at Aucharroch

Harold had brought him in to the fields to give him a better chance. When I saw him in the field we call Foreburns, he was standing on top of his mother's back, and her lying, but when we got near enough we saw she was dead. That moment I restored the balance between triumph and absolute despair. Somehow the 722 acres with their weed-free pastures and immaculate crops lost their savour and all I was was a 59 year old cripple standing beside the dead mother of his best tup lamb. The mood persisted in me all through the evening meal and when the Thomsons left for home I said, "Well Colin, what's doing with you?"

"Jim," he said, "It's some years now since I asked you to look out for a farm for me; there's not room for Roy and his family and me and mine on Keillor; please try and get something for me."

I sat looking at him, he had been a pal ever since schooldays and was always helping other people. I heard myself as in a dream. "Colin, do you think you could manage Aucharroch? I'll give it a count up and tell you the price tomorrow at 6 o'clock. Take your dad over it and if you can pay what I ask it's yours."

Next night I asked for £289,000, excluding the Border Leicester flock which Marcus is to get. Like Jim Gammell ten years before John McLean answered, "Jim, you're not asking too much, anyway we will just take it."

So I bought the house I am in now to live in and the crofts of Bridgend of Balloch to keep me from going mad and for exercising Fred, and another chapter of my life had begun.

CAPITAL PUNISHMENT ON GROUNDS OF PROBABILITY OF GUILT

You know how about every ten years when some particularly brutal murder or series of murders occur, there is a public demand for the restoration of the death penalty in various dimensions. Some say a life for a life, some want the death penalty for premeditated and not for spontaneous murder, some want it for political assasination, some for terrorist killing, others for killing policemen — betraying state secrets — you name the crime and it has its advocates. Some 90% of us belong to one or other of the pro lobbies, but of course hardly anybody believes in every one, and most of us would differentiate between the murder of an eight year old schoolgirl, abducted on her way home, sexually assaulted and then strangled, and the distraught father who happened to catch said abducter at the scene and battered him to death with a pickaxe handle.

The most cogent argument against the death penalty is of course "but what if we hang an innocent man?" — it being often overlooked that the female of the species can be just a vicious and callous as the male, and often even if they do not personally bump off the victim they are the incitement behind the deed.

I have always been a pro death penalty person, and even although I believe there have been persons convicted and put down who have apparently been proved innocent of that crime, usually by a so-called confession by some other criminal trying to sell his life-story to some newspaper, I feel that many more innocent lives would be saved if those who contemplated murdering someone knew what was in store for them if they were discovered. Nevertheless this story illustrates how it is possible to pass judgement in error.

Most people know that if you waken a red deer calf which you have happened upon sleeping in a clump of rushes or heather, how it will follow you home no matter how much you try to get away; and how young lambs will rush underneath your tractor or Landrover if you surprise them out of a sleep, and all you can do is to shut off the engine and wait till their frantic mother re-orientates the little fellows with much murring and nuzzling and conducts them away to safety. Many's the collie who has had to thole being attacked by a maddened Blackfaced ewe because her lambs had mistaken the innocent canine for their mother. This is one indignity that Fred endures, he seems to understand and gives ground though it's queer how he does not extend his concession to cattle if they attack him; they get bitten no matter the circumstances.

The other preliminary to this story is the behaviour of a bereaved ewe which should tell an experienced shepherd the likely cause of the disappearance of the lamb. If the lamb died in some place of concealment such as a large rabbit burrow, or in a crevice amongst boulders, the ewe will run to the spot where she knows it is and threaten a dog or person who approaches. If the lamb is visible but dead, she will scrape it with her forefeet to attempt to get it to rise, and will continue this behaviour for several days. On the other hand if she has had her lamb taken by a fox she resigns herself immediately and rejoins the flock without a backward glance. Some people say you cannot get such a ewe to take another lamb that year but I have managed it more than once although they tolerate the substitute rather than love it.

Anyway, a few years ago I bought a Blackface shearling at Stirling from Drew Provan of Parkhall, after David Brown the herd told me its mother was nine years old and a particular favourite of his. He had remarkably bright, alert eyes and his every movement indicated pent-up energy, ready to be released, the very thing one looks for in a hardy hill breed. I gave him seventeen ewes, amongst which were a pair of nearly identical twin sisters, just eighteen months old, gimmers to sheep men. They were very close as well as very alike, always grazing together and even in the buchts they were invariably in the same pen. Sure enough one forenoon in mid-April they each had a single tup lamb, not one hour between them and again as like as two peas. They both sucked without assistance and I left them at darkness down for the night in the shelter of the fir wood about one hundred yards from the Quharity river. As I always separate the newly lambed ewes from those who are not yet lambed to prevent thieving and mis-mothering and naturally look at the unlambed ones first in the morning, it was after I had breakfasted before I went to check up on yesterday's crop.

There were the two sisters grazing peacefully together as usual about three hundred yards from where I had left the night before and when I went to get their lambs they made no attempt to follow me and never even gave a bleat. Although I looked the area where they should have been I knew I would never see them alive again and in seething anger I set out at once to locate the den of the guilty party. Discovering a fox's den with cubs in it is not a particularly difficult job if your nose is efficient and the wind is right, for the combined stink of fox itself and the stench of the rotting carcasses of its victims betray its presence from 200 yards. Within an hour I got what I was looking for, just a few yards from the top of a steep bank in a wooded ravine cut through the hill by the Quharity in some bygone age when the world was cooling down. I took off my jacket and laid it at the entrance to keep whoever was in at home, then went and alerted Peter Gillon of my discovery.

Peter is the gamekeeper on Pearsie. He does not like foxes or cats, and is wise in the ways of the wild. As dawn was coming in next morning he imitated the call of the vixen to her mate and shot him dead when he approached. Having eliminated any chance of retribution, Peter then gassed the earth and went home for his breakfast. In the afternoon, out of curiosity I pulled away the divet he had used to block the entrance and there she was, lying dead and with a dead cub in her mouth. I felt that I had been a good shepherd in the very best tradition, and though I had lost two lambs I knew the rest would be safe. Can you imagine my feelings when Peter phoned one dinnertime about a week later, "Jim I had a look along the burnside where we killed the foxes and took two dead lambs out of a pool, I put them at the door into the steading."

Reader, I suppose you know the rest. It was them all right, and I knew what had happened. Their mothers had taken them down to the burn with them where they went for a drink, they had lain down and slept on the bank, wakened and seen the moving water, jumped in and been carried away. I had overdone the genes which are responsible for nervous energy. Although the tup's mother lived till she was nine, her son did not pass on to his progeny the instinct of survival. If there is very little between genius and madness, the over-provision of the ingredients of self-preservation can mean self-elimination. Everybody save Peter Gillon is a loser in a case like this, the tup was killed and eaten and his horns made into stick heads, the gimmers lost their lambs and the joy that mothers have with their young, the family of foxes lost their lives completely innocent of the crime of which they were accused, and every time I think of the devoted mother trying to save one of her children even as she choked to death I have an uncomfortable feeling that I offended against some unwritten law of decency which we hope would operate if we were in other shoes.

I hope Alick Buchanan-Smith does not read this story — or he will demolish me next time we argue about capital punishment.

HOW BEAUTIFUL IS SCOTLAND

I think it would be about 1952 that I and three companions took a three-day tour of the North of Scotland to see how the North College's direct seeding of hill land, particularly heather, was faring. The new idea of each seed being coated with its own fertiliser needs sown amongst heather stumps intentionally left by burning with the wind, held much interest for me, for it made possible the improvement of steep faces too dangerous to improve, using the traditional plough and discs.

Each of us had served in the war, all in different branches of the armed forces, so there were not many parts of the world that one of use was not acquainted with. George, now Lord Mackie of Ballinshoe, had distinguished himself in the Air Force; Ben Coutts, equally in the Gunners; Ray Legg in his New Zealand Infantry, and myself in the Armoured Brigade — although, as readers will know, my contribution was limited.

Ray had come to Britain to complete his education, I think in chemistry, on a Fison's scholarship. I cannot recall under what circumstances he was with us, but with the self assurance of most of those from "down under," he made himself so completely at ease, one would have thought we had known each other all our lives; and the constant stream of jokes and reminiscences was only interrupted when we were at our food, when our mouths were otherwise engaged. Ben, of course, had suffered horrific facial war-wounds, with the result that much of his present face had originally been some other part of him, and had been transferred by the supreme skills

of some of our surgeons, by grafting. Ben is, of course, an ac-
complished after dinner speaker, and to demonstrate the camaraderie
which existed amongst us, and still does, I instance a Kirriemuir
Agricultural Association dinner where George, as chairman, introduced Ben. After a short resum of his career to date, George con-
cluded "And if you think he is an ugly bugger now, you should have
seen him before the Germans tidied him up."

On our trip one of the stops we made was to examine a 16th century fridge which was a cave that had had its open end walled up
and had been packed with ice taken from the river which flowed
alongside. The compartment so formed had been filled with meat
and salmon. Ray was deeply impressed. "They sure knew how to
live at that time," he said, "and off what nature had provided them
with too." Then, because I was the nearest, "Jim, do you know how
to survive in the Arctic circle?"

"No, Ray, I don't," I answered, "but I am sure you will not leave
me in such an appalling state of ignorance, for you can never tell
when I may find myself alone and ignorant amongst the cow caribous
and the seals."

"No, no," quoth Ray, "you are further north than that in the
land of the polar bears, your only source of food or clothing, so
listen carefully, till I teach you how to catch them."

"As I said, you will be on an icefield, and first you must make
your ice axe and chip away till you cut through the ice a 4' round
hole, taking care not to break the centre bit which is known as the
"ice lid." Lever the ice lid out of the ice hole, roll it away twenty
yards, leaving it on the edge. Then take a tin of peas and place a
pea every four inches all round the very edge of the icehole. Then
go and hide behind the ice lid and sure enough, you won't be there
long before a bear comes down for a pea. Wait until he has his back
to you, then rush up behind him and kick him right in the ice hole."

So far I have not had to put my newly acquired knowledge into
practice, but knowledge is at least easy to carry.

Late afternoon next day we had to stop as the roadway was oc-
cupied by a lorry in process of being loaded with trees, which were
being transported to it from a bing on the felled area of woodland
nearby. It was some three-quarters loaded and the driver, perched
on top, made no effort to dismount and shift it to let us past, and
we realised that he was not intending to do so until it was loaded
and secured. We were right up beside it, and Ray said, "I wonder
if I could persuade him to let us past?"

Strolling casually up to the side of the lorry he addressed the driver
in a friendly and cheerful way. "My good man, have you ever had
a kick in the balls?"

When the driver replied in the negative, Ray's voice and manner suddenly changed and was charged with menace and violence. "You won't be able to say that again, my boy, that is unless you have that ..... lorry on the side of the road thirty seconds from now." He looked at his watch, but by this time the driver was in his cab and moving. Ray got into his seat beside me in the Rover. "I always thing it pays you to be nice to people," he remarked, "what an obliging fellow that is."

That evening, after our meal in the hotel we were staying in, we were cracking in the lounge. Ray waxed eloquent about his good fortune in life, so I will try to relate his story in his own words, as near as I can.

"When you are a child in New Zealand, if you are of Scottish descent, from the time you understand speech, you are subjected to a never-ending indoctrination of the unsurpassable beauty and the glorious history of Scotland and its people, depicted at Burns night, clan gatherings and get- togethers of any kind, by song, recitation, bagpipe music or Highland dancing, until you have built up in your mind a land of scenic magnificence, populated with heroic men and lovely women.

"By Yon Bonnie Banks, Dark Lochnagar, Ye Banks and Braes, O' A' the Airts, Ae Find Kiss, Tam O'Shanter, The Cottar's Saturday Night — all these and more so impressed the minds of the children, that it is their dearest wish that one day they will be lucky enough to visit the land of their forefathers and pay homage where it matters most. Imagine then my joy when I won my scholarship and was able to realise my fondest dream.

"I was able to stand on the very spot where the stag had drunk his fill before bedding down in Glen Artney's shade. I could visit Loch Leven where the prettiest of all the Scottish Queens had been held captive, I could visit Loch Lee churchyard where rest the remains of Alexander Ross, poet and historian extraordinary, with his memorable epitaph on the headstone.

How finely Nature aye be painted
For sense and rhyme he ne'er was stinted.
Straight frae the heart he always sent it
Wi' might and main.
And no ae line he e'er invented
Could ane offend.

"These, and Bannockburn, Stirling Bridge, Flodden, Culloden, — God, I would be able to savour my birthright.

"You know, chaps, at first I was more than a little disappointed. At home we have bigger lakes — you call them lochs — than Katrine or Awe; we have bigger mountains than Nevis or Cruachan; some of the rivers you sing about I've seen some fellows doing more against a wall after a night on the beer. We have mists on the braes, too, at home, and the moon on the hill as well. O.K., we don't have heather or thatched cottages at burn sides, but we have some wide span bridges and fine buildings, mostly the work of engineers or architects of Scottish origin. That's when you suddenly realise that it's here it all began. The people who wrote the songs and the poems glorifying Scotland wrote them before New Zealand was about, and they lived and died knowing only their own land, and building up this picture of Heaven being not very far from lovely Stornoway.

"When you look again, now, with your eyes opened, the real Scotland is there to worship and you wish that the poets and writers of bygone days had been able to paint even a far lovelier picture of the land that created and supported us, but of course that is not possible, there are not any words fit to describe the beauty and majesty of Scotland."

He stopped and looked at us in turn, "Gee, chaps, I'm some proud to be one of its children."

Ray, if you ever read this, so am I.

Portrait of the Author by Joyce Grubb 1981

POEMS

A LITTLE GOES A LONG WAY

On the night of the Policeman's Dance in Brechin
Everybody was ready for the "hoochin":
The guests turned up to indicate
They thought Tayside Police were great.

The leader of this worthy force
Had promised to attend, of course.
His presence there on such a night
Was both enjoyable and right.

Along with Frank and Muriel Young
The Littles joined the merry throng.
The meal was good, so was the wine,
And everything was going fine.

Alas — across the car wireless
Urgent and frantic S.O.S.
The message came the chiefs to tell
Things in Montrose were all to hell.

It seemed that some villain had entered a shop
And with a short shotgun had threatened to drop
Anybody who tried to prevent him from taking
All manner of foodstuffs from biscuits to bacon.

The next thing he'd done was to hijack a car,
One with enough petrol to travel to Ayr,
Where he and the bird that was there for his use
Had decided to kip in her half brother's house.

And what made the whole thing a bloody sight worse,
At the point of a gun and with physical force
He'd abducted two people with methods inhuman,
One was a man and the other a woman.

What he wanted them for God alone knows.
(He'd been watching the telly too much, I suppose).
By this time the whole Police Force was alerted
And efforts to catch the mad rascal had started.

SEL-LA-V

Towards Dundee at breakneck speeds
The captured driver who must needs
Obey each order that he got
Is forced to drive or else be shot.

His hapless wife sat in the back
The shotgun pointing at her neck,
And soon they were at Broughty Ferry
And still he ordered "Hurry, Hurry."

The mad career came to a stop,
Rammed by an outraged plain clothes cop
Whose training had caused him to think
The driver was the worse for drink.

Before he could say "What's your name?"
The gangster's weapon spouted flame.
Thank God he missed; none was hurt.
For cover cop and driver spurt.

Left with the thugs the helpless wife
Was in great danger of her life,
Tied to the gun in such a way
That kept the tough police at bay.

For in his hand he held a cord
To trigger off the gun secured.
And had he fallen or been drowned
Discharge it must, with fatal wound.

This thing had got to such a state
It seemed right to negotiate.
To see if there was any way
To save the lass from injury.

When all this lot was going on
Who should arrive but Frank and John.
Said Sergeant Melville to the thief
Would you like to natter with "the chief?"

The rogue said it was his ambitions
To mix with men in these positions,
And to get the proper atmosphere
Would somebody bring some cans of beer?

This was no sooner said than done,
Negotiations then began.
Said John, "This is a sad affair,
Half of my force is standing out there,
Traffic held up as far as Errol
And threatening harm to this poor girl."

Replied the crook, "I want to Ayr
And Miller has to drive us there.
Agree to that and you come too
I'll swop the silly bitch for you."

Says John, "If what you say's sincere
We'll start as soon as Miller's here
And to eliminate delay
We'll get an escort all the way.
And if we get a good clear run
We should all be in Ayr by one."
(o'clock in the morning that is).

And as he said, by one o'clock
In Ayr's town square the cars did stop.
Two shots rang out, the thief had fired,
The dashboard of the car destroyed.

No sooner was the gun discharged
Than John the villain overpowered
Until at length with help at hand
The bandit was secured and bound
And removed to the nearest pound.

The happy ending to this story,
Rewarded for his night of glory,
John got from our dear sovereign's hand
The highest honour in the land.

For such a brave and daring deed
Let all the people of Tayside
Rejoice, for when the chips were down
And danger threatened, *we had John.*

SEL-LA-V

BALLAD OF HENRY McGINN

Now this is a story that needs to be told
But it's coorse to know where to begin,
But there must be a place, to record the disgrace
Concerning Henry Fisher McGinn

Chorus
McGinn, McGinn, it's paid you to sin
£6,000 we've got to give ya,
I wish to God your Judge had been
Gaddafi out in Libya.

McGinn was a Fireman in the City of Perth
Who developed a thirst as he sat at his hearth,
But he didn't like buying his whisky and gin,
He used more simple methods to get the stock in.

Now a dignified bishop had parked his car,
It was not his intention to go very far,
And he wouldn't be long, it was surely all right
Not to bother to lock it, there was no one in sight.

He didn't see Henry concealed very handy
Devoured by thirst for religion and brandy,
While there on the back seat, was just what he'd need:
The spirits to guzzle, the Bibles to read.

At this stage I think it's only but fair
That everybody should know how stuff like that was there,
Some believed he had bought it in a grocer's shop in Balbeggie
But it was really a present from Lady Carnegie,
A prominent member of his congregation,
Who, like Henry, well knew that there were two kinds of spiritual
consolation.

So he nabbed what he needed and set off for home,
But the Bishop returning saw what was goin' on
And unfrocking in haste, he took up pursuit
With a view to applying the toe of his boot
As well as, of course, re-possessing the loot.

Uplifted no doubt by religious belief
He was rapidly closing the gap to the thief,
Who in sheer desperation discarded his hauls,
For he dreaded the thought of a kick on the leg.

Now his strategy worked, for the Bishop drew rein
Giving thanks most devout, for his treasures regained.
But he counted his chickens before they were hatched,
The books were unharmed, but the bottles were snatched.
(There seemed one consolation, McGinn had been catched).

"£5 do I fine you," said the Beak looking severe,
"And count yourself lucky that it's me that's up here,
But I am treating your case as a temporary lapse
For I think Tayside Fireman are excellent chaps."

But Firemaster Jones took a different view
And he said "All my men must be clean through and through
And to keep you, a thief, on the Tayside Brigade
Would destroy all the trust up to now that we've made,
So I sack you at once, Henry Fisher McGinn
Never darken the door of my office again."

Do you think that our Henry was full of remorse?
Not a bit, and to law he took instant recourse,
And most strongly complained that his sacking was rough
And the fine of £5 was, he felt, quite enough.
He had not even managed to taste the damned stuff.

Chorus 2
If in Tayside you should live
Here's the best advice that I can give,
However honest you may feel,
Never buy what you can steal.

So a Tribunal was called to look into the facts,
Under one of those crazy Industrial Acts
Designed by some madman the Unions to please,
Who have managed to bring Britain down to her knees.

Three people accepted the invitation
To pronounce upon the whole situation,
Possibly inwardly reflecting in a state of bliss,
"We should be able to knock £60 apiece out of this."

Our trio were at pains to say
Alf Jones behaved impetuously
And did not use the normal channel
And lots of other legal flannel,
And 'cos it was a first offence
He should have had another chance
And on them the impression that Jones had made
Was he thought he was running the Fire Brigade.

The damages they then assessed,
And as you have already guessed
They named the sum £5965
To help McGinn to stay alive
In the style of life to which he had become used,
And which in their opinion he had not abused.

McGinn could scarce believe his luck,
He really didn't care a great deal about the money as long as his
character was cleared.
He would have been quite pleased with a fiver,
Because he'd now got a job as a lorry driver.

As a result of the findings of the three
We in Tayside, except those in receipt of Social Security,
Have now to pay six thousand pound
To compensate the thieving hound.

It is to be hoped that before very long
We will be able to distinguish right from wrong,
And adjust our laws to make Tayside
A place for decent folk to bide.

"I was so overcome with the beauty of the Glens I had to write the
enclosed poem, which you are at liberty to use."
Dr A.B. Ross to Dr McCantley

THE GLENS OF ANGUS

The glens reach out like fingers
and point towards the sky
To show the way to paradise
for travellers such as I.

SEL-LA-V

Shee, Esk, Lethnot, Prosen
Isla and Clova too,
Are lovely glens of magic
Always with something new.

A partridge or a pheasant,
Shy deer upon the hills,
Quiet cows and sheep in meadows,
and little bubbling rills.

They wander to the rivers,
That gleam amongst the trees;
While high up in the mountains
Are alpine flowers to please.

The following verses have been added by the author.

And forty little rabbities
Sit basking near their holes,
While great big heaps of new dug earth
Betray the busy moles.

I envy not their daily task
Of digging for a meal,
I'd rather be an otter or
Even a flippin' seal.

And only swim about the sea
When the water's nice and warm,
And live on salmon and sea trout
Proceeding up the burn.

There is one risk in being a seal
A fate most horrible,
What if you happened to be born
The year there was a cull.

Imagine lying on the beach
Contented and serene,
When some .... belts you with a club
Direct between the e'en.

It would be coorse to have to live
Just skulking in the dark,
I'd rather be some sort of bird
Especially a lark.

Then far above the clouds I'd fly
And sing my sweet refrain,
I'd sing until my wings got tired,
Syne I'd come doon again.

Even being a cow would be O.K.
Contented with her lot,
But it would be just like my luck
To have to be a stot.

So having got my Ph.D.
(This dream of mine) I must forgo it,
Whatever I would like to be
I'm certainly not a poet.

So next time I am in your glen
Before I start to use my pen
I'll try to mind to count to ten
And no write dross like this again.

Amen.

APPENDICES

Linrie
Kirriemuir
Angus
Scotland
4-8-80

The President of Egypt
Mohammad Anwar El Sadat
The Presidential Palace
Cairo

Dear President

Now that the dust has settled and the world is focussing its attention on new matters of international controversy, one glorious action from the tragedy of Iran will remain for ever in history, and
that is your part in it. Alone amongst world leaders you have followed the path of honour and dignity living up to, and even exceeding
the legendary heights of statesmanship displayed by your mighty
predecessors who ruled your nation in the early days of civilization.
On behalf of the millions of people throughout the world who have
been uplifted and inspired by your actions I salute you, great man,
you have by your deed rightly taken your place in immortality.
May God be with you and your people.

James Findlay

Written on the occasion of Egypt granting asylum to the deposed
Shah of Persia, after he had been betrayed by the Western Nations
who had encouraged and supported the policies which caused his
downfall. My letter was not acknowledged. JF

Case for Local Authorities Support for Animal Diseases Research Association

Sixty years ago people with human and animal welfare at heart formed the Animal Diseases Research Association and purchased the land on which the Institute still stands. The object was to undertake research into diseases affecting farm animals, identifying the causes and discovering the optimum treatment. This Association has developed steadily over the years and has achieved world-wide recognition as a leading one of its kind. Our Scientific Director and senior staff members are known internationally and liaise with their fellows in similar posts in the continuing battle to control ills which have, over the centuries, impoverished great areas of the world. A significant proportion of the Association's work is carried out in collaboration with medical researchers in the fields of foetal, nervous, enteric and dentition disorders. In these areas animals have parallel disorders to those found in humans. Many of the diseases which afflict humanity are of course transmitted from animal or bird sources.

Apart from the benefit to human health from the successful control of human plagues such as malaria and sleeping sickness, there is the obvious bonus of a more plentiful supply of animal products on which depends the standard and quality of nutritional protein and natural fibres which in turn determine the well-being of the nations. The victims of the lack of such provisions so vividly being portrayed in television programmes about Cambodia, Uganda and other countries are proof enough of what happens when society forgets its priorities whilst our own people equally demonstrate how scientific research devoted to a good cause ensures the maintenance of a healthy and happy environment for all to enjoy.

Although much of the Association's work is funded from Government sources additional money is always needed to enable us to keep on top of the ever growing need and demand as proliferation in human and animal terms adds new stresses and complications which trigger new strains of bacterial and viral infections. The current freer movement of people and animals adds to the ease by which many diseases spread by contact, e.g. rabies.

I am sure that the people of Scotland, known for centuries as caring people for animals, would wholeheartedly support their local authorities contributing to keep their own Institution in the forefront of this vital world service.

A contribution of £1 per 1,000 population would ensure this objective and would be amongst the best investments of all the grants made by local authorities to outside bodies. My own Region has in fact already agreed to contribute on this basis.

James Findlay, Tayside Regional Council,
Director, Animal Diseases Research Association.

Extract from Dundee Advertiser, Friday Sept. 24, 1880.
Glenisla Cattle Market, Tuesday

This annual market was held today in a convenient field to the North of the Hotel. The weather was dull and drizzly and at times rain fell but did not prevent the satisfactory transaction of business, though the rather unfortunate circumstance of the sale of the select herd of the Earl of Strathmore happened the same day preventing many parties from Strathmore being present, still there was a large attendance of farmers, dealers and graziers. Gentlemen were on the ground from a great distance, the Lothians, Fife, Perth and Forfar shires; whilst some of the extensive purchasers were there from Dundee, Perth and other towns. As a result of the system springing up in the Glen of parties disposing of the stock privately previously — a course generally condemned — the number of cattle exposed was not nearly so numerous as last year. From 300 to 400 were exposed. Most of them were two-year-old polled Angus stock. From the highly favourable past summer, with the exception of one or two lots, the whole animals were as fine specimens of store stock — close, beautiful, fat and in superior condition — as could be found in any locality in Scotland. During the past few weeks the value of young stock has been steadily on the increase. Combined with the rich aftermath and the large crop of turnips, the demand was very animated. In a short time every lot found purchasers at an increase in price compared with 1879, of from 30s to 40s per head, which highly pleased the holders. The Forter, Craighead, Newton and Beloty lots were amongst the largest and earliest sold. Messrs Johnstone, Perth obtained about 100 head; Mr Sime, Fife nearly 40; Messrs. Easton and Fife, Forfar about 20; Mr John Adam, Castleton of Eassir, Messrs. Miller, Dundee and Mr. Alexander, Alyth were good buyers. Best cattle realised from £20 to £23, secondary from £12 to £19, and inferior lots from £14 to £15 per head. Fat cows brought from £19 to £21. Several milch cows were sold at from £10 to £15. Stirks fetched at from £7 to £9. The following were the chief sales — Mr. James Jack, Forter sold lot of bullocks at £21 to Messrs. Miller, Dundee; second lot of queys at £18 to Messrs. Johnstone, Perth; a third lot of queys at £16 and fourth lot of queys at £16 to the same parties. Messrs. Stewart, Craighead sold polled lot at £23.10/- to Messrs. Miller and lot of stots at £17. Mr. John Robertson, Glenshee sold lot polled cattle at £19 to Mr. John Adam, Jun., Tarves. Mr. Nicoll, Daldo sold lot of stots at £21 to Messrs. Eaton & Fife, Forfar. Mr. John Milne, Clachknocketer sold lot of 6 polled stots at £19 to Mr. Sime, Fife. Mr Thomas Adam, Shonly, Lintrathen, sold 8 stots at £16 to Mr. Alexander, Alyth. Mr Ferguson, Carle sold 7 stots to Mr. George Rough, Courtachy at £16. Mr. Charles Storrer sold lot of polled cattle at £20 to Mr. Sime. Mr. David Ogilvy, Easter Hall, Lintrathen sold lot of 3 queys at £40 to Mr. Wylie, Glassburn and another lot of 9 bullocks at £19:10/- to Mr. Fife, Putmuies. Mr. Fleming, Blackwater sold lot of stots at £19 to Messrs. Johnstone. Mr John Robertson, Runavey sold lot of polled at £19:10/- to Mr. Adam. Mr. Graham, Dalvanie sold lot of stots at £20 to Mr. Walker, Forfar. Mr. Fleming, Blackwater, sold four stirks at £24 to Messrs. Wallace, Auchinleish. Mr David Lyon, Newton sold lot of 12 stots at £21 to Mr. George Nicoll, Southmains, Forfar. Mr. Small of Diranean sold lot of polled stirks at £12 to Mr. Thomas Harrison, Inchmichael. Mr. William Wilson, Auchrannie sold lot of 8 stots at £15:15/-. Mr Peter Robertson, Blackwater sold lot young cattle at £16. Mr. John Anderson, Glenmarkie sold cow off the grass at £21. Several foals and young horses were offered. Few sales of them took place. Mr. William Robertson, Miller Kirkton, Lintrathen sold one foal at £10.